*The Masters' Secrets*

of

# TURKEY

# HUNTING

by John E. Phillips

Book 1 In The Turkey Hunting Library
by Larsen's Outdoor Publishing

ISBN 0-936513-18-7

Library of Congress 91-76443

Published by:

[OP]

LARSEN'S OUTDOOR PUBLISHING
2640 Elizabeth Place
Lakeland, FL 33813

PRINTED IN THE UNITED STATES OF AMERICA

2 3 4 5 6 7 8 9 10

# DEDICATION

When my brother, my sister and I were young, she caught sparrows in mouse traps and baked them in a pie as a practical joke to feed my Dad and a nuisance friend of his who always showed up at dinner when times were hard. She allowed my sister, my brother and myself to expand our creative outdoor skills by mounting birds and animals in the basement as well as raising an alligator in our fish pond-- even when she thought we were weird. She worked most of her life to make our lives better and happier. Without her, this book would not have been possible.

Thanks, Mom, Rhoda Elizabeth Phillips, for all your help and support over the years.

# ACKNOWLEDGEMENTS

I am one of the luckiest men to have lived on this earth because I have had the opportunity to hunt with some of the greatest turkey hunters in America. Many of them have helped me with this book by not only sharing their secrets with me but also a portion of their lives on the hunts we've been on together.

Bringing words and photos together is no easy task either. I want to thank those who labored with me on this book -- my wife, Denise Phillips, Cara Clark, Mary Ann Armstrong, Marjolyn McLellan and Margaret Smith, and particularly Larry and Lilliam Larsen for their expert suggestions and fine layout and printing work.

A book is not written without inspiration. The inspiration that has fired me when my creativity has been cold is a young lady who through her personal life has shown the courage of a lion, the dedication of Job and the winning spirit of a champion, like Eric Liddle of "Chariots of Fire"-- Jennifer Ann Moyer, my fourth child. Jenny, I always knew you could!

Special thanks to outdoor writer/photographer Laurie Lee Dovey for her photo on the back of this book which captures the author in action.

# PREFACE

The wild turkey has woven a mystical, magical web around my life.  Because of the gobbling of *Meleagris gallopavo*, I went to college, missed the Vietnam War, met some of the finest sportsmen in America and have been able to earn a living for my family while enjoying the most fun a man legally can have.

In preparation for writing this book, I missed only five days of turkey hunting from March 10 through May 31, 1991.  I hunted with some of the true masters of the sport and added to my knowledge of gobbler chasing.

Hunting the wild turkey is the ultimate outdoor challenge. Chasing gobblers is similar to the game of chess in hunting, while taking any other kind of game can be compared to a contest of checkers.  But I must warn you that the sport of turkey hunting is infectious and can cause a lifetime addiction to the sport. However, you will learn in the last chapter of *The Masters' Secrets of Turkey Hunting* from the graybeards, who will tell you that you can hunt turkeys as long as you can walk or have someone carry you into the woods.

# TABLE OF CONTENTS

# ABOUT THE AUTHOR

For more than three decades, John E. Phillips has hunted the wild turkey. He even chose to attend Livingston University in turkey-rich Southwest Alabama to be able to turkey hunt at least four days a week from mid-March until the end of April during his college years until graduation.

Phillips also has been a student of turkeys and turkey hunting as a parttime taxidermist and an active outdoor writer and photographer for more than 20 years for both newspapers and magazines. Phillips, the author of nine outdoor books including: The Masters' Secrets of Deer Hunting, Alabama Outdoors Cookbook, How To Make More Profits In Taxidermy, Catch More Crappie, Outdoor Life's Complete Turkey Hunting, Bass Fishing With The Skeeter Pros, North American Hunting Club's Turkey Hunting Tactics, Deer & Fixings and Fish and Fixings, has had more than 600 articles published on turkey hunting. An active member of the Outdoor Writers Association of America, the Southeastern Outdoors Press Association, the Alabama Press Association and Outdoors Photographic League, Phillips has won numerous awards for excellence in writing magazine and newspaper articles and outdoor books.

Phillips feels fortunate to have hunted with some of the greatest turkey hunters of our day, which has made him passionate for the sport. He has taken turkeys with blackpowder rifles and with shotguns. He has hunted the mountains, plains, swamps, forests and croplands of the U.S. Phillips has learned the art of turkey hunting from many hours in the woods and from some of the best hunters in the nation. He brings this knowledge to you in The Masters' Secrets of Turkey Hunting.

# CHAPTER 1

# LEARNING FROM
# PhD GOBBLERS

"How did you learn to turkey hunt?" a friend asked one day.

"I learned from the masters," I answered.

The friend, knowing I had hunted and worked with some of the best turkey hunters of our day, assumed I meant those men.

But these masters of the sport are only upperclassmen in the school of turkey hunting. The true doctors of turkeydom are the professors who earn the degree, Masters of Turkey Hunting.

## Fred

Fred, my first teacher, wasn't a very smart turkey, but I wasn't a very smart hunter either. I met Fred just off a backwoods road near the Tombigbee River in West/Central Alabama. I was in college at Livingston University at the time where a fraternity of turkey calling and hunting addicts resided.

Like most fledgling gobbler-chasers, I had heard all the stories of legendary turkeys and the tactics used to bag them. My friends at college showed me how to call turkeys on a Lynch Jet slate box turkey call I had bought. For weeks, I practiced with the call. When my buddies commented on how the calls I was making were good enough to bring in a tom, I took the Jet and went into the woods to hunt gobblers, without any further instructions.

Unknown to me, I was following a philosophy taught by one of the gurus of turkey hunting-- Lovett Williams of Gainesville, Florida. In later years, Williams told me his philosophy of turkey hunting was that the best way to learn to hunt turkeys was to buy

13

a call, go into the woods and hunt. Williams explained, "The turkeys will teach you the rest of the sport."

Apparently, I luckily had stumbled on the right way to learn to turkey hunt. Walking down an old logging road where I had seen turkeys when I was deer hunting, I decided to sit down and call. I didn't sit by a tree or build a blind, since I hadn't learned about the importance of either as yet. I sat down in the middle of the road and started making noises on my slate box.

After waiting 20 minutes and neither seeing or hearing anything, I got up and started sneaking down the road. When I had gone only 40 yards, I heard something walking. I squatted down. In six heartbeats, I saw a real, live, wild turkey walking straight to the spot from where I had been calling. I couldn't believe my eyes. Because the turkey was going directly to where I had been, I must have called him to me. But I had gotten up too quickly. I hadn't given the bird time to come to me. The tom never had gobbled, although I always had heard that turkeys would gobble. This tom walked so straight and erect he reminded me of a friend named Fred.

Fred, a corporal in R.O.T.C. at my high school, had been proud of his position. He was ever-conscious of his stately, upright posture. I was fascinated by how tall the turkey, Fred, looked coming through the woods. But as I watched, Fred kept getting further away.

"I've got to shoot that bird," I thought as the bird was at 40-yards, headed straight for my calling position. I took aim and fired at the whole turkey, instead of at his head. Learning to shoot for the head at 30-yards or less would be another lesson for another day.

When I fired, Fred took to the air. I fired three more times before Fred dropped on the other side of a backwoods slough off the river. Because I thought I heard the turkey across the water, without hesitation, I hit the water. This turkey was my first one, and I meant to capture him if I had to fight tigers or wade water. The frigid, early springtime water moved up to my armpits as I held my gun over my head. Only later did I remember I had forgotten to remove my wallet before I plunged into the water.

On the other side of the water, I saw a downed tree where I was sure Fred must be. I reloaded and made my assault. Apparently I had guessed right. When I walked into the top of the blown-down tree, Fred ran out the other end and once again took to the air. Although I fired three times, Fred kept gaining altitude. When he

*In this small head, the gobbler has enough knowledge to defeat most hunters.*

was 50 yards away, he lit in a large water oak tree. Probably he was tired of this ground action.

"I'm going to get that turkey," I told myself. "This fight will be to the finish."

Staying behind the downed tree, I belly crawled on my stomach in the mud of the swamp.

"This is war," I decided. "I'm in college and smarter than any ole turkey. I can outmaneuver this bird and take him."

I had crawled about 20- to 30-yards when I saw Fred getting nervous and fidgeting on the limb.

"I've got to take this 50-yard shot," I told myself, even though I knew a 50-yard shot with a 2-3/4-inch 12-gauge was risky at best. However, I thought I was well-informed about trajectory, velocity, distance and speed. With my infinite wisdom, a belief held by most college students, I thought I could judge just how high I should shoot over the bird's head to effect a kill-- even if the pellets did lose velocity and drop during flight.

I aimed about 18 inches over the tom's head and squeezed the trigger. The gun exploded, but Fred remained sitting in the tree.

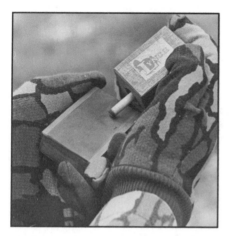

*The little Jet slate call was my first turkey call.*

Evidently Fred hadn't pinpointed from where the sound had come and was not leaving the security of the limb until he did.

"I held the gun a little high," I thought.

I lowered my bead to 12 inches over the turkey's head and fired again. This time Fred decided he had endured enough of my brilliance and flew off into the pages of turkey hunting history, never to be seen or heard from again.

I couldn't believe I hadn't taken that turkey. I was smarter than him, had more firepower than he did and totally was dedicated to my cause. Besides, I was wet up to my neck and coated in swamp mud. I deserved to take Fred home to dinner. How could I have failed? For weeks, I dreamed about the mistakes I had made.

On that first turkey hunt, I learned that ...

... turkeys often come in silently in the afternoon.

... you should sit next to a tree bigger than your shoulders for back cover.

... 40-yards is too far for a 12-gauge, 2-3/4-inch shell to effectively and consistently take a turkey.

... a turkey in a tree is home-free. Shooting a turkey off a limb carries a worse social stigma than stealing from the poor.

... patience takes home more turkeys than brilliance ever will.

... one hunt is not enough to master the sport of turkey hunting.

### Elmer

This bird was the chairman of the certifying board from which all gobblers received their PhDs. He was absolutely brilliant--the kind of turkey each of us must hunt before we have our masters' degrees in turkey hunting conferred on us. Elmer was a legend that had been hunted and shot at by several fine turkey hunters. However, no one could kill the bird.

A turkey like Elmer is much like the gunfighters of the Old West. Many may challenge them, but only one can defeat each one. A gobbler like Elmer tests the mettle of a gobbler chaser. This type of tom knows who you are, what you want to do and how to avoid you. But if you can take an Elmer, your name will be written in the history of turkey hunting by all those who've tried to bag this bird but have failed.

Elmer was a good gobbling turkey that would gobble from the roost just before daylight to taunt hunters. But at fly-down time, he would become as silent as a church mouse. To hunt a tom like Elmer, I determined I must first do some research to learn all I could about the bird.

I discovered that most of the hunters who challenged Elmer had used a mouth diaphragm call. I decided to call with a slate or a box--hoping the turkey might work better to those calls since he had heard them less frequently than the mouth diaphragm.

Because Elmer would answer a call before daylight, I found out that most hunters had called aggressively to him with cuts, cackles and loud yelping early in the morning. I determined to hunt Elmer from 10:00 A.M. until dark using only soft clucks and purrs. I hoped to give the gobbler a call he hadn't been hearing much at a time of day when he hadn't been hunted too hard.

The most popular camo pattern in this area was woodland green, and many of the men who had chased and trained Elmer to dodge hunters had worn this pattern. Although I couldn't prove my ideas, I believed turkeys that saw the same camouflage frequently might be able to identify it in the woods. I chose to wear a vertical pattern with more brown lines.

Next, I wanted to know where Elmer fed, strutted and traveled. No one had been able to take Elmer hunting him like a turkey. Perhaps I could find the chink in his armor if I hunted him like a deer. If I learned his daily routine, I should locate a spot in the woods where he felt safe and to which he normally and naturally would come. But that site had to be a place where Elmer never had encountered a hunter. Finally I made the decision not to hunt Elmer more than one week, because a bird like Elmer could be a season-wrecker.

I hunted Elmer for five days. One morning I saw Elmer. When he was at 30-yards, I put the bead of my shotgun on the white

*The PhDs of turkeydom wear feathers instead of shirts and beards rather than ties.*

wattles of his neck. Just as my index finger found the trigger, I slid the safety off my gun and slowly applied the slightest pressure to the trigger. However, just before the gun reported, Elmer stepped behind a tree. Then like the ghost of the forest he was, Elmer vanished without a sound.

The next day, I went to Elmer's strutting grounds. I successfully called the turkey to within 50 yards. I watched him strut and drum on a knoll in a hardwood bottom. The tom could see in all directions for 80 yards.

Even though I was camouflaged perfectly and hadn't called too much, Elmer would not come to me. Elmer had learned that if a hen was as close as I sounded, he should be able to spot her. If he couldn't see her, at least she should have been able to see him and move to where he was. Without that visual contact with his hen, Elmer wasn't budging.

I scratched in the leaves to simulate a hen's feeding, and I purred like a contented hen. Elmer still would not leave his strutting ground. Finally, I let the stubborn tom walk off and live to play the game again on another day.

Although I saw Elmer at some time every day I hunted him, I never did get a shot at that smart bird. But I did learn my lessons well.

... Take the first, good shot you have at a gobbler. More than likely, he'll never give you a perfect shot.

... Have some type of obstruction like a hill or a ridge between you and the turkey, if the gobbler is an old tom. Then when the hen doesn't come when the turkey gobbles, struts and drums, the bird may move to a spot where he can see her, and you can bag him.

Some gobblers like Elmer never will be killed by a hunter. These turkeys are quick and smart enough to have earned their PhDs in hunter dodging. In daily combat with all manner of predators, both two-legged and four-legged, these birds have won the prizes and have their doctorates in teaching those who try to master turkey hunting.

# CHAPTER 2

# THE 10 SINS OF TURKEY HUNTING

**With Preston Pittman**

Most turkey hunters defeat themselves in the woods, because they commit sins that spook turkeys. From watching turkeys and turkey hunters most of my life, I've learned how to disguise many of these mistakes. You can too. The entire time I'm in the woods, I'm trying to think like a turkey and make the sounds of a turkey.

Let me emphasize that many of these strategies are tactics I use only on private lands when no other hunters are in the woods. Remember, I'm trying to sound like a turkey. Because these sounds are what other hunters are listening for, if you employ any of these techniques, be very cautious.

## Sin No. 1 - Spooking Turkeys When You Walk

I try and change the noise I make when I'm walking through the woods from human noises to turkey noises. I want to sound like a hen as she goes about her daily routine. Turkeys take erratic steps and don't walk with a regular cadence like a hunter does. Usually I take three steps, wait, take one step, wait, and then take four steps when I'm walking in the woods hunting turkeys.

I also cluck and purr as I walk and scratch in the leaves with a cadence by using my foot. If you've ever watched turkeys scratch in leaves, the scratching has a definite rhythm of scratch; scratch, scratch; scratch. The clucking and purring are the contented sounds hens make as they feed.

*Preston Pittman of Lucedale, Mississippi, has won the world's Natural Voice Championship more than any other caller. The president of Pittman Game Calls, not only can Preston think like a turkey, move through the woods like a turkey and call like a turkey, but many believe he even looks like a turkey.*

When I come to a dusting site, I pat the ground with my hand or seat cushion to sound as though a turkey is dusting. If I'm walking through an acorn flat, I'll move much slower like a turkey that's feeding. If I'm walking through a pine forest, I'll generally walk somewhat faster.

## Sin No. 2 - Coughing Or Sneezing

I always carry a deer grunt tube with me into the woods. Then if I cough or sneeze while turkey hunting, I can blow the grunt call to cover the sound of the cough or the sneeze with a deer sound, which often is heard in the woods. Or, I can turn that cough into a drumming sound, if a tom is in close to me. When you're listening to turkeys, notice you'll often hear a sound similar to a cough when gobblers drum. If I don't blow the deer grunt call or make the vrooooom of a drumming sound after I cough, then I immediately give a cluck or two to cover that cough. Never make a human sound around turkeys without covering it with a turkey sound.

## Sin No. 3 - Swatting Mosquitoes or Scratching

I keep my hands close to my body and move my hand very slowly to the place that needs to be scratched or to the mosquito that must be swatted. I make the swat with two fingers rather than my whole hand. After that, I brush my shirt sleeve against the side of a tree to make a sound similar to what a turkey's wing sounds like as it walks through the woods and brushes the side of a tree.

## Sin No. 4 - Making A Bad Call

To hide a bad call, continue to call. Never stop calling when you've made a mistake. If you listen to turkey hens, you'll realize they often call poorly. If you hit a sour note, keep on calling, and then you'll probably sound just like a hen. The gobbler won't remember the sour note you hit. But if you stop on that sour note, the tom will think about that last, bad note and possibly be spooked.

## Sin No. 5 - Being Spotted By A Turkey

If I'm in the woods and a turkey sees me, I stand still and try to resemble a stump. If I'm in an open field, I'll lie down on the ground and hope I blend in with the dirt.

If you're carrying a decoy with you like the lightweight and collapsible Feather Flex decoy, you'll totally confuse a gobbler that has seen you if you reach into your pack, get that decoy out and slowly and carefully put it in front of where you're lying. That tom may not know for sure what's lying in the field, and he certainly won't understand from where that hen (decoy) has come.

As I'm putting the decoy up, I start clucking and purring to sound like a hen turkey. I sometimes will tilt the decoy over so she looks like she's pecking. When the gobbler hears the sound of a hen clucking excitedly and sees her feeding in the middle of the field, I think he forgets all about seeing me and comes to investigate her. If you don't have a decoy, then lie flat and pray. Be sure to check your state's regulations on using decoys for turkey hunting.

A gobbler has a keen sense of curiosity. If he doesn't know for sure what's lying in a field, many times he may walk to within 30 yards or less just to see what you are. Then you can take the shot.

## Sin No. 6 - Overcalling

Usually a hunter doesn't realize he's called too much to a bird until the tom stops at 50 to 60 yards and refuses to come any closer. When this happens, wait until the gobbler can't see you, and then change locations and callers. If you've been calling with a mouth diaphragm, use either a slate call or a box call. If you can't move, wait until the tom walks off. Then make a big circle, attempt to get in front of the turkey, and call to him again.

*Crawling is a tactic Pittman often uses in the woods when he has to slip up on a turkey.*

## Sin No. 7 - Being Caught In A Poor Position

Often a hunter will roost a turkey in the evening and return to that bird before daylight. When the tom gobbles the first time, the hunter may realize he's less than 40 yards from the bird and must sit down immediately where he's standing. A situation like this means you must pull out all the stops and become a turkey hunter rather than merely a turkey caller.

When I'm this close to a gobbler, the only calls I'll give are soft, contented purrs. I scratch in the leaves lightly and brush my shirt up against the side of a tree to duplicate the sound of a feeding hen brushing up against a tree.

*If you can hide the sounds you make so a gobbler doesn't know whether he's heard a human sound or a natural sound, then you won't scare him.*

If the tom is gobbling a lot from the roost, I take the opposite tactic. I cut, cackle and call aggressively. Often that gobbler will fly and light within 10 feet of me, or else he'll come running to me when he leaves the limb.

The key to success is to let the tom tell you how to call to him when you're in close. If he's only gobbling a little, then give him the soft, subtle calls of purring, scratching in the leaves and brushing your shirt up against the tree. If the gobbler hasn't shown up after 15 minutes, hit him with some aggressive cutting and cackling. Make him think a party's going on and he'd better come join it.

## Sin No. 8 - Missing An Opportunity To Take A Shot

Sometimes when a turkey comes in, for one reason or another, you can't take the shot. Maybe a twig is between you and the bird, or perhaps he steps behind a tree before you're ready to shoot. Or, maybe you can't get the bead on the bird in time to make the shot.

Once the bird has passed by you and walked out of sight, circle, and get in front of the bird. Knowing where a turkey wants to go and where he likes to be at different times of the day may result in your having a second chance at a gobbler if you miss the first

*As you walk in the woods, brushing your clothes up against the side of a tree can sound like a turkey's wings brushing that same tree.*

opportunity. Be sure to make a large enough circle to get in front of the tom without spooking him.

If the turkey has been gobbling to the call you've been utilizing, then start off with that call. However, if the gobbler doesn't answer you, change calls on your second attempt.

## Sin No. 9 - Spooking A Tom

When you spook a turkey, continue to call. The sounds a tom makes when he's spooked are the same sounds-fast clucking, wings beating and running in the leaves--he makes when he's excited. When you spook a bird, cut at him, cackle to him, and call excitedly. Even if you flush a gobbler, cut and cackle to him, because these sounds are excited calls.

Other turkeys in the area that hear the tom fly off and those excited calls you're giving may think the gobbler is flying into you rather than away from you. Attempt to turn scared sounds into excited sounds to make other turkeys come in to where you are.

## Sin No. 10 - Shooting And Missing

If you shoot and miss, then start giving a cutting call quickly before the smoke clears the gun barrel. Because turkeys regularly hear thunder in the woods, the turkey you're aiming at may think that loud blast is thunder. If you start cutting immediately after you shoot, you'll sound like an excited hen that also has been spooked by the thunder but is waiting for the gobbler to come to her. Don't move after you shoot and miss. Then you'll totally confuse a tom.

Approximately three out of 10 times, that same gobbler will come right back to you. If the turkey has gobbled and responded previously to the call I'm using, then I'll continue with that same call to try and get him back. If he doesn't return within 30 minutes, I'll move, circle, get in front of him and utilize that same call with more pleading in it to attempt to call that same turkey again.

Turkeys make mistakes just like hunters do. Because turkeys can be confused, often a tom will wonder if he's seen and heard what he thinks he's seen and heard. By confusing a gobbler or convincing him he hasn't seen or heard you, you often will be able to take many of the birds you normally spook. To hide the 10 sins of turkey hunting, think, talk, and act like a turkey when the sin is committed.

# CHAPTER 3

# MASTERING THE CALLING SECRETS OF THE PROS

The masters of the sport of turkey calling consistently take more birds than most of us do because they've developed secret tactics to force gobblers to come in -- even when the toms don't want to respond to calling. These little-known secrets have enabled these master hunters to return to camp with turkeys on their backs when most of us are empty-handed. Let's listen to the techniques of the masters to improve our abilities to bag gobblers.

## Terry Rohm

Terry Rohm has learned to hunt turkeys from the Far North to the Deep South.

"I believe most hunters try to take a stand and call a gobbler over too great a distance," Rohm explains. "If you're hunting turkeys in areas with high hunting pressure, the gobbler will not walk very far to find a hen, because he knows he's more likely to run into a hunter than he is a sweetheart.

"Another problem with calling from 150 to 200 yards away is you may be attempting to call a tom over an obstacle the bird doesn't want to cross such as a small creek, a big ditch or a fence you can't see. I try to get as close to a turkey as the terrain will permit before I call to him. I'll crawl through a small ditch or stay on the other side of the hill from a bird.

"Many times I'll spend two or three hours trying to outmaneuver a gobbler before ever calling. I'll move around thick cover and use whatever terrain breaks I can to hide my movements until I get within 50 yards of the turkey.

*Terry Rohm of Madison, Georgia, the PR director for Wellington Outdoors, the producers of Ben Lee Calls, has finished in the top five in the World Turkey Calling Championship and has won the Pennsylvania State Calling Championship several times.*

"Then I'll give some soft yelps. Often I'll surprise a gobbler, and he'll either gobble or come in silently. Perhaps when you get that close to a turkey without his knowing it and you give some soft calls, the turkey thinks, "I can't believe that hen is right there, and I haven't heard or seen her. I'll just walk over and check her out." Then that's when you can take him. When I call, I want to be ready to shoot.

"Hunt the turkey first before you start calling. Get close, and call softly. More than likely, you'll be able to take even the toughest toms."

## Allen Jenkins

Allen Jenkins, another longtime master turkey hunter, says, "Patience will kill far more turkeys than award-winning calling will. I've found most hunters tend to call too much, get up too quickly, walk off and leave the gobblers coming to them. If you've

*Allen Jenkins of Liberty, Mississippi, the president of M.L. Lynch Calls, is a longtime avid turkey hunter who judges many turkey calling contests and is a master woodsman.*

ever watched a turkey walk through the woods, you know the bird may move very slowly. If a turkey is not fired-up about mating, he won't be in a big hurry to respond to your calling.

"The key to knowing when to call is understanding when not to call. If a turkey answers your calling, and then after 15 minutes you call again, and he gobbles the second time closer to you, the turkey is coming. Leave him alone! Don't call anymore!

"Because all a turkey call is supposed to do is make a tom come to you, don't talk to the bird when he's on the way. Even if he picks up some hens, if he knows where you are, sooner or later he'll come to you. For instance, when you call to a gobbler on the roost, and he answers you but doesn't come in, you either can stay at that spot or return to that same place at 10:00 or 11:00 A.M. The gobbler may come to you then. As long as you don't call too much to a turkey, he usually will find you eventually if you wait long enough. If you want to bag more birds this spring, call less, and wait more."

## David Hale

David Hale has a deadly technique for unhanging hung-up gobblers.

"A tactic I've used for the last three years to take turkeys that will not come in is to lie flat on my stomach," Hale reports. "Then I start clucking with either a pushbutton box call or a mouth diaphragm call.

31

*David Hale of Cadiz, Kentucky, the co-owner of Knight and Hale Game Calls, is a master caller. Hale also moves through the woods like a cat, calling numbers of turkeys, not only for himself but also for other hunters each season.*

"When I get the turkey's attention, I take my fingers and throw leaves up in the air like a hen does when she's scratching. Even if the gobbler sees you, most of the time he won't spook because you're below his eye level. When the tom spots those leaves flying below eye level and hears a hen calling but can't see her, generally he's curious enough to come over and find out what's kicking up those leaves. Usually a gobbler won't come in strutting and drumming but will come in clucking. I lie with my gun in front of me, which means I'm very limited as to how much I can turn or move to take the shot.

"One of the problems associated with this strategy is that sometimes the turkey will circle before he comes in to where you are. Then you must look out of the corners of your eyes to see where is he and to know when to take a shot. But I've used this method successfully to bag hung-up birds in recent years."

## Preston Pittman

Preston Pittman says, "The wild turkey has a language. To communicate effectively with a bird, you have to understand the language as well as the sounds turkeys make. A call consists of rhythm, pitch, tone and mood. Unless you give the right ingredients of each one, you won't be able to call in a gobbler.

"I compare the language of the wild turkey to human language. If I'm calm, cool, collected and relaxed, I usually speak softly and slowly in a low tone. If I'm excited, I generally will talk louder and faster--depending on how excited I am.

*Kelly Cooper, one of the masters of turkey hunting and the owner of Kelly's Kallers, has been involved in the outdoor industry for more than 20 years. Cooper understands how to make calls and how to use them to seduce gobblers.*

"When a turkey talks to you, or you talk to that turkey, you must understand his mood. If you can't change his mood, try to match his mood with your calling. If a fellow whispers softly into a girl's ear, more than likely she will not scream at him. If she does, she's going to cause him to retreat, back off and hush. But if she whispers sweet nothings into his ears in the same mood and tone, more than likely they both will accomplish what they want.

"If a fellow is walking down a beach, sees an attractive young lady in a bathing suit and yells to her, 'Hey you good looking thing,' and she yells back, 'Come on over and see me,' then they are both communicating with the same pitch, rhythm, tone and mood. This understanding draws them closer together.

"You've got to talk to a turkey the way he talks to you. If you cut and cackle to a gobbler, and he gobbles back immediately and very aggressively, then you know he is attracted to your calling, excited and willing to come to where you are. But if you cut and cackle to a gobbler, and he gobbles in a hushed tone like he's trying to gobble under his breath or waits several seconds before he gobbles back, then he's not in an aggressive mood. You must change your calling style with more seductive, less-aggressive calls.

"A cracking or a barking type of call usually denotes excitement. A slow, soft, easy call generally means the bird is not very excited.

If you'll learn to match the mood of your calling to the moods of the turkey you're attempting to call, you'll be far more successful at bringing in gobblers."

## Kelly Cooper

Kelly Cooper is one of the veterans of the sport and has many longbeards hanging from his lodge pole.

"The young gobbler's squealing call, also known as the kee-kee run, can be very deadly on springtime longbeards," Cooper advises. "Most turkey hunters assume the kee-kee run is only a fall call. But often a call that's totally unexpected for a time of year will be the one that will pull in a longbeard when nothing else will work. Because the kee-kee run is high-pitched, the pitch alone may trigger a gobble. The kee-kee run is also a distress call, which may cause a gobbler to come and investigate.

"Another reason the kee-kee run brings in gobblers in the spring is because this call is given by a young turkey. When the hens in an older gobbler's harem hear a kee-kee call, the call triggers a mothering response in those hens. They will come to investigate and pull the mature gobbler with them to you.

"Many hunters fail to realize that the kee-kee is one sound hens make, especially young hens, besides being the young gobbler's squealing call. Many times when an older tom hears a young hen giving that kee-kee call, he thinks he has a fresh young thing he can move in on quickly and mate.

"A few falls ago I was out turkey hunting. I had busted a flock up the night before and started calling in the morning. I had a tom come to me making no sounds but a kee-kee and a coarse gobble behind it. When I shot the bird, I discovered he was a four year old gobbler with 1-3/8-inch spurs and a 10-inch beard. This experience taught me that old gobblers, as well as hens and young gobblers, can and will kee-kee. Oftentimes that's the call I can take a bird with in the spring when nothing else works.

"Another tactic I'll use, especially if I have a hung-up turkey, is to give some fast, loud, fighting purrs, rake my hand through the leaves and pat my chest like turkeys fighting. Many times when nothing else will break a gobbler out of a strut and make him come to you, simulating a fight between two gobblers will."

Most of these techniques are unusual but are some of the tactics the best turkey hunters in the nation use. When you have an older gobbler that won't respond to your calling, these strategies may help you take your bird this spring.

## CHAPTER 4

# KNOWING WHEN TO MOVE ON TOMS

To move or not to move--that is the question. Many of us who hunt turkeys fail to answer this question correctly. About 80 percent of the mistakes made when turkey hunting occur when you either move too soon or don't move soon enough. Here's a look at two of the nation's best turkey hunters with different styles of hunting who will share with us when to move and when not to move on toms.

### How To Stay Put And Double Dip

Every year I go to Liberty, Mississippi, to hunt with my friend, Dale Faust. Although Faust and I have chased numbers of gobblers together for many years, each season I learn something new from Faust, who's been an avid turkey hunter all his life.

One morning, Faust had located several gobblers roosting across a small creek from us behind some thick cover.

"These birds usually fly down into this open hardwood bottom and walk up on the ridge in front of us to gobble and strut right after daylight," Faust informed me as we cleared away the leaves in the dark from the base of a tree where we planned to set up. "I believe if we take a stand here by this big chestnut oak we'll get a gobbler and be gone before 8:00 A.M."

Just before daylight, Faust began to call, and three turkeys gobbled. As the sun slowly brightened up the sky and promised light for a new day, I heard the toms fly down out of the trees and land in the dirt road just above us. Faust gave a few soft yelps and whispered, "Get ready."

With my Browning 5A-automatic resting on my knee, I waited for the turkeys to appear. In less than five minutes, I saw the tri-colored heads of three longbeards bouncing down the road toward us. The gobblers were on the run to what they thought would be a hen ready to be bred. When the birds were at 20 yards, Faust clucked to stop the procession. As one of the toms stepped away from the group and craned his neck to see where the hen was, I fired. The turkey tumbled.

"Don't move, don't move," Faust cautioned me urgently but quietly. "Stay very still."

Instantly Faust started to cut and cackle like an excited hen. Although the other two gobblers were spooked, they only ran about 10 to 15-yards before they stopped, looked back and tried to determine what had happened.

"Shoot one of those other gobblers," I told Faust.

But before Faust could get off a shot, the two turkeys walked off. Faust decided he would bag one of the gobblers-- if he could call the bird back in to where we were set up.

"How can you possibly hope to call a gobbler back to the same spot where he has seen his brother die?" I asked.

"Since lightning often strikes in the woods, and turkeys are accustomed to hearing the loud clap of thunder and seeing the white flash of lightning, maybe if we don't move, those two gobblers never will know we've been here," Faust suggested. "I believe I can call at last one of them back."

Faust explained that one of the biggest mistakes turkey hunters make is moving after they shoot.

"Often if you miss a bird, if you'll stay still, and the bird doesn't see you, you can call that same turkey back to you," Faust reported.

But I hadn't missed. My gobbler was 20 yards away on the ground. When I brought this fact to Faust's attention, he answered, "I still believe I can call those turkeys back, if we'll just wait on them and spend some time hunting them."

The two gobblers had moved to their strutting ground on top of a nearby ridge. When Faust called, the toms answered with gobbles. However, now the gobblers had hens with them, because we could hear the hens yelping, cutting and cackling.

As I told Faust why we never would get those gobblers away from the hens, he responded, "We don't have to, John. I'm going to give up on calling those gobblers. Instead I'll call the hens. If we can pull the hens off the ridge, the longbeards will follow them."

*Dale Faust of Liberty, Mississippi, knows when to move on turkeys and even can get in close enough to take them with a bow.*

After Faust gave some aggressive cuts and cackles, the toms and the hens answered. Faust mentioned that, "We'll have to wait these turkeys out. If we give them enough time, I think we can get the gobblers to respond and come back to us."

Usually I've moved on turkeys in this situation, changed calling positions and calls and tried to make the gobblers come to another area. But Faust, who hasn't found success moving on turkeys, is convinced the odds are two to one against you any time you can hear a turkey, and you make the decision to get up and move.

According to Faust, "Our best chances to kill one of those gobblers is to pull them back to the place where they've been this morning."

The sun was beginning to climb high in the sky at 10:15 A.M. Faust and I had been sitting in the same spot since before daylight. Although we already had been successful, now we were trying to have a super hunt by bagging two gobblers under the same tree on

37

the same morning without moving. As I thought about the magnitude of the feat we were attempting, Faust once again cut and cackled like a demanding boss hen. Instantly his call was answered with cuts and cackles, which made Faust think he had the dominant hen's attention as he cut and cackled again. The war of the calls went on between Faust and the dominant hen for about 10 minutes as the hens came closer and closer to us.

"I see her," Faust whispered at the same time I spotted the blue head of the hen.

While we watched, the boss hen, with eight more hens following behind her, came looking for us. Off in the distance, we observed the white crown of a strutting, longbeard gobbler moving toward us. With the hens all around us, the wait for the tom seemed eternal. I even squinted my eyes to keep the hens from seeing the whites of them and being spooked. At times, we had hens within six to 10 feet of our blind, as the boss gobbler steadily came to where we were set up.

When the longbeard stepped behind a tree 40 yards from us, Faust brought his three inch magnum to his knee and prepared for the shot. The turkey came to us until he was at 38 steps. Then he putted and craned his neck. He appeared not to like something about our blind. As I felt the tom was preparing to run, Faust's shotgun reported. The gobbler crumpled in a pile of feathers.

On the way out of the woods that morning, I started to question Faust about when to move on turkeys.

## Why To Stay Put

"I believe you increase your odds of bagging a bird by at least 50 percent if you'll wait on a gobbler instead of chasing him," Faust said. "Instead of thinking of all the reasons why you can move on a tom, you'll be better off if you'll start considering why not to move on a turkey, including ...

... the gobbler's hung up,

... a creek or a brush pile is in the tom's way that he won't cross,

... the turkey has hens with him,

... the bird is call-shy,

... I'm set up in the wrong place or

... I'm too far from the turkey.

"Your mind will continue to play games with you. Very rarely will you consider that...

... the turkey just may be walking slow,

... you need to wait more and call less to bring in this bird,

*If you move at the wrong time on a gobbler, you'll spook more turkeys than you take.*

... the tom realizes you're in the woods, and you need to let him find you,

... your best chances of killing the gobbler are to wait him out rather than chase him down, since everyone else who's hunted this bird has chased him but hasn't killed him.

... you must not move, since the turkey probably will see you,

... the bird may have pinpointed where you're calling from and

... a gobbler can see further in the woods than you can."

Faust believes the sport of turkey hunting is as much if not more a mind game than it is a hunting experience. One of the strongest urges in anyone's mind when he's hunting any game is to move. We always believe when things don't happen as quickly as they should that we can move and speed up the action. But when we move, more than likely a gobbler will spot us.

"I'm convinced the hunter who wants to increase his odds of bagging turkeys should rarely if ever move on gobblers once he starts to call," Faust emphasized.

Faust and I didn't move on our hunt and bagged two longbearded gobblers at the same site on the same morning.

"And maybe if we had a third hunter with us and continued to sit still, I could have called that third gobbler back to us before dark," Faust commented.

## High Pressure Hunting

"I have to try and produce a gobbler every day for the sportsmen I hunt with," Bo Pitman, lodge manager of White Oak Plantation near Tuskegee, Alabama, told me. "I move on turkeys a lot. I feel the key to bagging a gobbler is not necessarily in my ability to call but rather is in my knowledge of what a turkey prefers to do and when he wants to do it. I try to outthink and outguess turkeys. I believe if you can be where a tom wants to be before he reaches that place and bag him when he comes to you, you have to be a much better hunter than if you solely rely on your calling ability."

Pitman considers understanding the turkeys and their habits and knowing the land he hunts as absolutely necessary to his being successful when he uses his run-and-gun tactics. Because Pitman live on the land where he guides turkeys hunters, he knows every tree, blade of grass and bush by its first name. He's familiar with each roosting site, dusting area, watering hole and strutting zone on his land. Pitman also studies the turkeys on his land before, during and after turkey season at various times of the day to learn where they go, what they do and when they do it.

## How To Run Toms Down

"If you want to kill a turkey and are willing to do whatever is required to get your gobbler, usually we will bag a bird," Pitman said on the first morning of my hunt.

Before daylight, we had gone to the base of a hill and listened. Just before dawn, a turkey gobbled.

"Let's go," Pitman instructed. "We've got to get to that tom before he flies down."

We ran up the edge of a dirt road and headed into the woods to set up on the gobbler. Pitman called several times. We heard the turkey fly down and gobble coming to us. But for some reason, the turkey wouldn't come to where we were. After a 20 minute wait, we backed out of the woods the same way we had entered. Staying close to the ground and moving as quietly as possible, we circled the tom, got above him and tried to call to him. However, apparently the bird had seen us move, because he never gobbled.

*Every day of turkey season, Bo Pitman, lodge manager of White Oak Plantation near Tuskegee, Alabama, guides clients to gobblers. He hunts the longbeards very aggressively.*

Walking fast and jogging occasionally, we covered the ground quickly until we came to the edge of a field. Pitman gave three yelps. A turkey gobbled just over a hill in the middle of the field.

"If we stay behind this hill, we can move up to the edge of the woodline and attempt to call the turkey out of the field to us," Pitman suggested.

However, when we started moving down the road, we had walked less than 50 yards before we spotted a gobbler, and he saw us. The turkey ran down the road before taking to the air. By now the time was 9:30 A.M. I felt our chances of bagging a turkey were somewhere between slim and non-existent.

But Pitman commented with a big smile spread across his face, "Don't stick a fork in me, John. I'm not done yet. A field about 3/4 mile from here always has turkeys in it. I believe we still can get one in the middle of the day."

As we went at a forced march pace toward the field, Pitman mentioned, "These turkeys come out into the field to feed, strut, bug, dust and mate. But when the sun gets high in the sky, and their dark feathers start to heat up, the heat of the sun will force them out of the fields and back into the woods to locate shade. We'll be waiting on them."

When we arrived at the second field, Pitman and I climbed down in a 1/2-mile long ditch running along the top of the field. As we belly crawled up the ditch, Pitman cautioned me to, "Stay low, and be quiet."

After a 50-yard crawl, we eased up to the edge of the ditch. Using our Nikon Mountaineer binoculars, we noticed that at least 40 birds were in the flock, which included seven longbeards and half dozen to one dozen jakes. Through our binoculars, we saw a band of three gobblers standing on a road. We watched as two of the toms fought and the dominant gobbler bred a hen.

"Let's move to the point of the field above the turkeys," Pitman said. "Then when the birds are ready to go into the woods, we can move and get in front of them."

We crawled back out of the ditch and made a 1/2-mile circle through the woods into the field so we would come out in the woods on the point of the field. From that spot, we watched for about an hour until the three gobblers began to move toward the woodline. Pitman mentioned he thought the birds were coming into the woods below us, and we needed to move once more.

We backed away from our observation point and traveled at least 250 yards into the woods before circling below the point where we had been watching the turkeys. I sat by the base of a large oak tree, and Pitman sat about 10 yards behind me. Pitman gave some light yelps, a few putts and a turkey's gobble.

While I watched the procession of turkeys walking, I knew Pitman had guessed right. Although I wanted to take the longbeard, when the lead gobbler got in front of me, he spotted me, craned his neck and began to putt. However, I already had the bead on the bird's neck. I squeezed the trigger. When I picked up the tom, I looked at my watch, which reported 11:30 A.M. We had seen turkeys all morning long, had the opportunity to call two and finally had bagged the third bird.

This run-and-gun hunt was one of the finest turkey hunts ever for me. As Pitman observed, "If you stay with the birds long enough and are willing to do whatever is required to take a gobbler, you can get your turkey."

## When To Go And When To Stay

Both Pitman and Faust are fine turkey hunters with their own styles that have been highly successful for each of them. You decide whether you should or should not move by evaluating your skills and knowledge of the birds and the land you're hunting.

*Knowing when to move and when not to move on turkeys is one of the most critical keys to success.*

To sit and wait on a turkey, you either must have a double dose of patience or else develop this skill. If you can't sit still for a long time and believe in your own ability to wait however long you must for a gobbler to come in, then you won't be as effective as you can be using this tactic.

You also must understand what a turkey is doing and why. For instance, if a turkey is with hens and won't come in, you've got to be able to call to him and make him respond. If the gobbler is call-shy, you have to know how to force him to come to your call. If the bird is across a creek or on the on the other side of a thicket, you must understand how to excite that tom enough with your calling to force him to cross that obstacle or wait long enough for the turkey to eventually come to where you are. You have to know when not to call, when to call and what calls to use as well as understand what's going on in the woods around you. You must outthink a gobbler and play mental games with him to make him come to where you are.

## To Run-And-Gun

To run-and-gun gobblers like Bo Pitman, you must spend time scouting, learning the lay of the land and determining where turkeys want to go and when they want to go there to aid you in planning your stalk and ambush. Observing turkeys at great distances with binoculars is another key to successfully being able to run-and-gun turkeys.

Also you've got to be in good shape to run-and-gun gobblers and be willing to walk three to 10 miles in a day of hunting. You must be certain how far you are from a turkey to know whether to run or to crawl. You must hunt an area with plenty of turkeys. Then if you do spook a gobbler, you can go to another bird before the day is over. You must be willing to wade creeks, climb mountains and belly crawl through mud or possibly cow pastures to get in position to take a shot. You've got to be able to outmaneuver a turkey and rely mostly on your woodsmanship rather than your calling skills.

Which way is best for hunting turkeys? This question can be answered only by you and your own personal philosophy of hunting. I've hunted turkeys both ways and found both tactics equally effective. Generally I let the knowledge of the land I'm hunting dictate the strategy I use. If I don't know the land and the turkeys on it, then I'll usually wait the gobblers out. If I'm familiar with the land, or I'm hunting with a person who knows the land, then I'll often run-and-gun gobblers.

To move or not to move is the question. Your knowledge of the birds and the land on each hunt you go on will give you the best answer.

# CHAPTER 5

# HUNTING PUBLIC LAND

### With Paul Butski

As the turkey approached, the ground shook with his thunderous gobbles. The bird was less than 100 yards and closing the distance fast.

Sitting beside a tree, I waited for the turkey to appear down the only path he could take to get to me. My head was low on the stock. My eyes were trained on the trail. My finger was resting on the safety, ready to push it to the off position and fire when that white crown appeared beneath the neck of blue and scarlet. However, about the time the bird should have shown himself, I heard the report of another shotgun less than 50 yards away.

"I can't believe what happened," Paul Butski of Niagara Falls, New York, said. "Another hunter got between us and the turkey."

Although I was madder than a wet hen, Butski soothed my anger with his words, "Hey, John, that's what happens when you hunt public land turkeys. The other hunter may have been set up on that gobbler before we arrived. That guy won, and we lost. Tomorrow is another day. We'll try to hunt a different bird."

According to Butski, public land hunting for turkeys is altogether different from private land hunting. "One of the main differences in hunting public lands in the North and private lands in the South is the way I scout. On public lands, I'll do most of my scouting from my truck. I may drive 50 miles in a day, stopping frequently to call and to see if I can get a turkey to answer me.

"When I hunt private lands in the South, I rarely drive the roads. Instead I spend most of my time walking and calling. In the South's heavy foliage, usually you won't hear a turkey gobble more

*Paul Butski of Niagara Falls, New York, is the president of Butski Game Calls, one of the nation's leading competitive callers and hunts gobblers in both the North and the South.*

than 100 or 200 yards. Also when I'm on private land, I must stay within certain boundaries, which are usually smaller areas than the public regions I hunt. So walking is a better way for me to scout."

Turkeys on public lands often will hear much more calling than turkeys on private lands since more hunters are trying to take them. For this reason, when you hunt public lands, you may want to change calls more often.

"I love to use the diaphragm call," Butski mentions. "However, when I'm hunting public lands, I'll use my box call and my slate call more often. The turkey I'm attempting to call to may have heard 10 diaphragm calls in the last three days. Because a box call and a slate call have a somewhat different pitch and tone from the diaphragm, if the gobbler hasn't heard those calls recently, they'll be much more effective than the diaphragm call."

When you're hunting private lands, rarely will you have to compete with another hunter for the same gobbler. But in New York, where Butski hunts state game lands almost exclusively, there is plenty of competition for each turkey.

Because Butski also guides on Southern Sportsman's Lodge lands in Alabama, he can compare the two styles of hunting.

"When you hunt public lands, you have to be much more aggressive and try and get closer to a tom quicker than you do on

46

*Butski calls from public roads to try and locate turkeys on public lands.*

private lands," Butski reports. "Since you must hunt more aggressively, oftentimes you'll spook more turkeys on public land than you will on private land. On private lands, I set up further away from a turkey when I start to call him than I do on public lands and take more time to work the gobbler in close enough to bag."

If Butski is hunting on the state lands in New York, as soon as he hears a tom gobble from the roost, he attempts to get near the turkey and call the bird to him before another hunter either reaches that same bird or gets between Butski and the gobbler he's hoping to work.

"Knowing and practicing hunter ethics is very important -- especially on public lands," Butski emphasizes. "If I spot another hunter's car parked in an area where I've heard a turkey gobble, I won't go to that bird. If I see or hear another hunter trying to work a tom I'm going to, I'll back out of that place and let the other hunter have the bird. But when I aggressively go after a turkey, I assume no other hunter is working that tom."

When Butski hears a turkey gobbling from the roost, he quickly makes a decision as to where the bird is and what the quickest way is to reach that turkey. He doesn't attempt to keep the bird gobbling on the roost once he hears him.

"If I've heard a turkey gobble, then more than likely another hunter has too," Butski comments. "I want to reach that bird as soon as possible and take a stand about 100 yards from him. I'll give a light tree call. If the turkey gobbles back, I won't call to him any more while he's in the tree. If that turkey answers the tree call, he knows where I am, and I don't want him to gobble any more to call in other hunters.

47

"One of the biggest mistakes hunters make is to overcall a tom while the turkey's in the tree. I'll let a bird gobble back to me several times without my calling to him, which usually will make him nervous when I answer him."

When a tom gobbles from the roost, he's calling the hens to him. The natural thing for a hen to do is to call back to the gobbler and go to him as soon as she flies off the roost. If a hen doesn't call back to the gobbler or go to him, the bird has a question mark in his mind. He's wondering whether or not she's found another sweetheart or what's causing her to not come to him. Maybe she's being flirtatious or coquettish. But for whatever reason she's not coming, the gobbler thinks all he's got to do is show his fine self to her, and she'll see the error of her ways.

Butski has found that turkeys on public lands are called to so much -- especially while in the tree -- that often a gobbler will wise up to the hunter's calling and stay in the tree until 8:00, 9:00 or even 10:00 A.M. before he flies down.

"Many times that turkey will remain in the tree and be silent, waiting to see a hen come in before he flies down," Butski mentions. "Since the turkey has shut up, most hunters will believe the bird has flown down and walked away from them. Then these hunters will walk into the roost site thinking the gobbler is not there and spook him off the roost."

However, when the turkey hits the ground, Butski changes tactics.

"Once the gobbler is on the ground on public hunting lands, I want him to come to me as fast as I can get him there," Butski explains. "I call with a lot of fast, sharp cutting and yelps like an excited hen to get the turkey fired-up and coming to me in a hurry. On private lands, often a hunter will quit calling and let the bird take his time to reach the spot where the sportsman wants to take him. But on public lands, you must continue to call until you're sure the turkey is totally committed to coming to you."

Yet another big difference in hunting public lands as opposed to hunting private lands is you have to hunt much more defensively on public lands.

"I won't deliberately compete with another hunter for a turkey," Butski says. "But this mistake is a common one often public land hunters make. No turkey is worth risking the likelihood of my getting shot. If I see another hunter's vehicle or hear another hunter calling to the turkey I'm trying to take, I'll back out of the area and let the other hunter have that bird. Most of the time on

*On public lands, you must take a defensive position to keep another hunter from sneaking in on you. If you spot another hunter, use your normal speaking voice to make him aware of your position.*

private lands, there's never a question of having to compete with another hunter."

On private lands, often Butski will move in close to a gobbling turkey that may be just on the other side of a ridge or thick cover. But according to Butski, "On public lands, you never try and sneak up on a turkey. I never get closer than 100 yards on a gobbling turkey on public lands. Accidents can happen on public lands when a turkey stands 100 yards or more away from a hunter and refuses to come to his calling. Then the sportsman may say to himself, 'I'm going to sneak in as close as I can to that gobbler and take a shot.'

"On public lands, often someone else may be working the same bird you are, which is why the turkey's not coming to you. When you sneak in on that gobbler, the turkey shuts up, the other hunter hears you walking in the leaves and sees what he believes to be a turkey in the spot where he heard the turkey gobbling. Then you may become a hunting accident."

Butski says the reverse scenario also can occur. "If you have a turkey gobbling to you, the bird quits gobbling, and then you hear footsteps in the leaves that sound like a turkey, you must assume those footsteps are being made by another hunter and are not a turkey coming to you. Not until you can identify clearly the head and the beard of a turkey should you prepare for the shot. The safest way to hunt public lands during turkey season is to assume everything you hear and see is another hunter until you are proven wrong."

Once you spot another hunter, give up the hunt. Accidents can occur on public lands when hunters see other sportsmen approaching and believe in their minds they can communicate their positions to the second hunter without spooking the turkey.

"Don't give a turkey call to attempt to get another hunter's attention so he'll see you and back out of your area," Butski emphasizes. "That hunter is coming into that region to see and hear a turkey. If he hears the sounds of a turkey, he may mistake you for a gobbler. Don't wave your hand, or throw sticks at him. The hunter who is coming toward you is looking for the movement of a turkey at about the same height you will be sitting at when you move. The safest and most correct action to take is to use your voice and say, 'Hey, fella, I'm another hunter. I'm over here.' You will spook the turkey, but you'll reduce the chances of a hunting accident."

Although some states are proposing mandatory hunter orange for the turkey hunter, Butski is convinced wearing the bright blaze orange will make bagging a gobbler very difficult.

"Rather than a mandatory blaze orange regulation, I favor a mandatory turkey hunter's safety course for all turkey hunters," Butski comments. "I don't believe anyone who hunts turkeys should be exempt from taking this course-- no matter how long a

*Make sure you see the beard on the turkey and clearly identify the target before you take a shot at a tom on public lands.*

person has hunted. We all can learn to be safer in the woods by completing a hunter education/turkey safety course. When you're turkey hunting, you're imitating the sound of the species being hunted. Therefore we have to be much more careful as turkey hunters than any other sportsmen who go into the woods."

Most of the turkeys taken in the United States are harvested on public lands that have plenty of good turkey hunting available. The good news is more and more public lands are being stocked with turkeys. However, to successfully hunt these areas, you may need to change your strategies and the calls you use as well as hunt aggressively and defensively.

# CHAPTER 6

# TOUGH TOM TACTICS OF THE PROS

The key to taking a gobbler is not your calling ability, your camo, the power of your shotgun or the number of turkeys on the property. To bag the toughest toms, you must know what a turkey is going to do before he does it.

One of the greatest turkey hunters who ever lived was "Uncle Roy" Moorer of Evergreen, Alabama. When I met Uncle Roy many years ago before he passed away, he gave me the secret to bagging even the toughest of toms. "All you've got to do to take any turkey, no matter how tough he is to hunt, is know where that turkey wants to go, get there before he does and let him come to you."

Uncle Roy's nephew told me, "The reason Uncle Roy has been able to bag over 500 turkeys in his lifetime is because he's always known what a turkey is going to do before the bird knows."

To take tough toms, you've got to understand the mind of the turkey.

## Henned-Up Gobblers

Preston Pittman not only can think and talk like a turkey, most sportsmen who know him agree he even looks like a turkey. The president of Pittman Game Calls, Pittman has developed three tactics for pulling in henned-up gobblers.

"The one technique that is talked about more than any other when you're attempting to take a tom with hens is to call aggressively by yelping, cutting and cackling loudly to the hen to try and get the dominant hen to pull the rest of the hens and the gobbler in the flock to you," Pittman says. "However aggressively that hen calls to me, I'll call more aggressively and louder back to her.

"Another method is just the opposite of aggressive calling but seems to work better when you're hunting an area where the turkeys have had a lot of pressure. When I know a gobbler is with hens in a high pressure region, I'll often give what I call sweet talk, which is very calm, quiet purring and soft yelping. Too, I'll scratch in the leaves with my hand. I'm trying to tell the dominant hen and the other turkeys in the flock with the gobbler that another hen is in the area, the feed is good and the region is safe and secure. I'm asking them why don't they come over and socialize. Turkeys are basically social birds. Many times letting a tom with hens know you're in a place can be much more effective in luring him to you than aggressively calling to the hen.

"The third strategy for reaching a henned-up gobbler is to forget about the hens altogether, speak directly to the gobbler and challenge him for his authority. I'll give some cutting sounds of the hen and gobble just as I finish the cutting.

"But be careful when you use this tactic because if there are other hunters in the woods, they are listening for that gobble. Only use this method when you can see very well or when you are on private lands.

"Many times when you challenge a tom by gobbling to him, and you make him think you're about to breed one of his hens, he can't stand the pressure and will come running at you. These three tactics have worked best for me when I find a gobbler with hens."

## Lock-Jawed Turkeys

A true turkey hunt is when you're hunting a turkey that doesn't talk. These lock-jawed gobblers are the specialty of Allen Jenkins, president of M.L. Lynch Calls.

"I like to hunt turkeys that talk very little and walk a lot," Jenkins explains. "These birds are at least four years old and usually have built up a reputation as being impossible to kill. To take this tom, you've got to know him better than your best friend.

"You've got to know where this lock-jawed gobbler is traveling and when he's traveling there. Before, I've even plowed the edges of fields, scraped woods roads with a bulldozer and cleared paths through thickets. Then when one of these toms that won't gobble walks through an area, I can see his track.

"Once I know where a tight-lipped gobbler is roosting, often I'll go before daylight, cluck to him once or twice and not call again

*When a gobbler is henned-up, if you'll just scratch in the leaves and call softly, you may be able to pull him away from the hens and into your gunsights.*

until I either see the bird or leave the woods. I may hunt him in the middle of the day, or I may hunt him late in the afternoon when no one else has hunted him. But the keys to bagging a bird like this will be patience, dedication, knowing where and when the turkey moves and doing very little calling.

"Lock-jawed gobblers will teach you how to hunt turkeys. They know much more than you do about the woods and hunters, or else they wouldn't have been able to survive for at least four years. Often I become so fond of these turkeys that given the opportunity to take them, I won't."

## High-Pressure Gobblers

David Hale of Knight and Hale Game Calls in Cadiz, Kentucky, reports that, "If a crook comes into your house and you know he's in the house, you'll go out the back door to keep from getting hurt or to get help. Then once the crook leaves the house, you'll return. Turkeys do the same thing. If there's too much calling pressure or hunting pressure, the turkeys will leave their homes (roost areas) and move to another region where they can see hunters coming.

"Turkey gobblers have certain regions where they strut, drum and are visible to hens without ever actually having to gobble. This same type of place is where a turkey can see a hunter approach. Often these strut zones are on hills or ridges where a tom can see all the way down the ridge and on either side of the hill. These strutting areas are the best spots to take a gobbler that is feeling a lot of hunting pressure because the turkey feels secure in these areas and can see the hens as they approach.

"One of the sites where I like to hunt these kinds of turkeys is where I can find two high points of land on a ridge with a saddle in the middle. Often a turkey will strut and drum on one high spot, walk down through the saddle and strut and drum on the other high point. If I take a stand in that saddle, I'll get a shot at the gobbler either going or coming. Even if a turkey doesn't gobble in the morning, he'll move to that strut zone and call his hens using strutting and drumming to let the hens know where he is. Many hunters don't understand a turkey doesn't have to gobble to get hens to come to him.

"When a hen is ready to be bred, she'll move close to that strut zone, especially when hunting pressure is intense, listening for the tom to drum and strut. When I get to the strut zone, I only call about one-tenth as much as I will in an area where the turkeys haven't been pressured. I'll usually cluck once or twice, perhaps give three soft yelps and then wait a full 10 minutes before I call again.

"I've watched gobblers in high pressure regions and am convinced that the least amount of calling I can do to let the turkey know where I am, the more interested the bird becomes in finding me. A gobbler will come forward two or three steps, strut and drum and keep looking for the hen. When he doesn't see her, he'll walk two or three steps and strut and drum once more. He's trying to get close enough to see her or let her spot him without actually having to commit himself to going to her. The key to taking this gobbler that is being pressured is to be patient. Don't rush the turkey into coming toward you.

"Most of the time when this tom finally does move to within gun range, you won't hear him. He'll sneak in to where you are and see you before you spot him. Remember, the turkey is dodging the hunter to survive. That bird will be as cautious as he can in hopes of seeing you first. The more you can become accustomed to seeing a blinking eye or the least movement of white and define a turkey sound, the more likely you are to see this bird before he spots you.

*Preston Pittman's soft calling tactics produce big gobblers like this one.*

"Turkeys don't leave an area when hunting pressure builds, and they become silent. They have nowhere else to go. You still can kill plenty of turkeys with a large number of hunters in the woods, if you'll pinpoint the toms' strut zones and hunt them."

## Walking And Talking Gobblers

Terry Rohm, PR director for Wellington Outdoors, mentions that often a turkey hunter may believe he has spooked the tom he's trying to take or someone else has spooked that turkey -- if the bird starts to come to you and then for no apparent reason turns and begins walking away from you. Generally you'll know this gobbler has been shot at before. He's attempting to come in close enough for a hen to hear him and then lead her away to a cleared area where he can see her to make sure he won't be shot at again.

"When a turkey is walking away from you and gobbling, don't use hen calls to talk to him to keep up with his location," Rohm advises. "Instead utilize owl calls or crow calls to keep the bird gobbling. Stay about 100 to 200 yards behind the turkey until he gets to a spot and stops. Then he's usually where he feels safe and secure and where he believes he can see a hunter or a hen approach.

*You may have to call a turkey like this one across a river to tag him.*

"The best way to take this turkey is to use the terrain to get in close enough to him to take a shot. Although some hunters call this bushwhacking, I don't. I think far more skill and woodsmanship are required to slip in close enough to take a shot at a turkey when you know he's looking for you than to call him in to a spot.

"Once a turkey reaches this safety zone, often he'll stay there for awhile. If you can't get a shot because the bird is at 50 to 75 yards, and you can't move any closer, then watch what the bird is doing. Generally that tom will walk back and forth in this safety

*Larry Norton, a turkey hunting guide at Bent Creek Lodge in Jachin, Alabama, and a member of Wellington Outdoors' Pro Hunting Team, won the World's Turkey Calling Championship in 1990 and 1991.*

zone. When he's looking away from you, give a very light cluck or yelp. I believe the gobbler thinks the hen is just out of sight and that she'll be able to see him and will come to him -- if he walks 10 or 20 yards closer. That's when you can take him. If you don't bag the turkey, then go back to that spot the next day. Don't even try to call to this tom when he's on the roost. Wait on the bird to move to you.

"When a turkey is walking away from you, he's going somewhere. To take that bird, you have to find out where that somewhere is and either bag him in the place where he wants to be or return to that spot the next day and wait on him to come to you. Remember, you don't want scare the turkey in this safety zone. If you do, probably that gobbler won't return to that same site during turkey season.

"If I call to a turkey in his safety zone, I use the Ben Lee Black Widow call, a single reed call with a soft rasp in it. You can blow it very soft and low and make the calls of a disinterested hen. All I'm trying to do with my calling is to get that gobbler to stick his head up over a bank or walk 10 or 15 steps closer to me.

"Hunting this kind of tom will require a double dose of patience on the part of the hunter. Just remember everyone who has been impatient with this bird hasn't been able to take him. Patience is your biggest ally. This turkey may take you on a long walk. Also you may have to remain motionless for an extended time. But that's the price you pay when you accept the challenge of hunting a walking and talking turkey.

"If this turkey had been easy to take, the fellow who had the first load of shot in the bird would have bagged him. Nine out of 10 of the turkeys I've finally bagged that have acted this way have had old shot wounds in them. I like to hunt walking, talking turkeys because not just any hunter can take them."

## Swimming Gobblers

When a turkey is across a river too deep to wade, you don't have a boat to paddle, and the river is too swift to swim, convincing that gobbler to swim or fly across the river can be a real challenge.

But Paul Butski explains, "Probably your chances are one in 10 that you can call that turkey. I know I did last year.

"To make that longbeard fly across the river, you must convince him there's more excitement on your side of the bank than on his side. So I do a lot of cutting, cackling and excited yelping. I use box calls, slate calls and diaphragm calls to try and sound like three or four hens are on my side of the bank that want to get bred. I give very demanding calls as if to say, 'Okay, ole boy, I know you're over there. However, we hens are over here. If you come to where we are, we'll have a party. But we're not going to fly to where you are.'

"Often you'll have to keep this calling up for a long to get an old gobbler to budge. Remember, as long as the turkey is gobbling, you've still got a chance to call him to you -- even if he's across a river."

## Hung-Up Turkeys

Larry Norton of Pennington, Alabama, is a champion turkey caller and hunting guide who deals with tough toms regularly.

"One of the hardest turkeys to call is a bird that hangs up and struts and drums 50 to 60 yards from you but won't come in to where you are," Norton reports. "Often hunters don't realize turkeys make more sounds than gobbling, yelping, cutting, cackling and purring. When neither the box call, the slate call or the diaphragm call will bring a tom to within gun range, I resort to using what I call turkey sounds.

"I'll scratch in the leaves like a hen and keep in mind that hen turkeys have a definite cadence to their scratching. They scratch two times, pause and then scratch one more time. Often this sound will bring a turkey in because he's already heard the hen call. However, if he doesn't hear her scratching or moving in the leaves, he will be suspicious and often will hang up. By scratching in the leaves, you can reassure the tom a hen is where he has heard the

*When a turkey won't talk, you need to know where he wants to walk to take him.*

calling. "Another tactic I use is to give a drumming sound like another gobbler with my natural voice. Many times when scratching in the leaves won't pull a tom in, the drumming sound will.

"If neither of those techniques work, I'll let the turkey walk off and move to another spot to try and call him. Oftentimes a turkey hangs up because he's been shot at or attacked by a predator in the place to which you're trying to call him. When you change locations, you can call him to a site where he's not afraid. I change calls when

I attempt to call a gobbler from a second calling spot. Sometimes you'll have to change locations two or three times to find an area where turkey will come. But when I'm really having a tough time with a turkey, I usually will use Ben Lee's Viper IV turkey call to try and bring in a tom."

Almost any turkey hunter can walk into the woods, hear a turkey gobble, sit down next to a tree, make a few calls and get the turkey to come to him. To learn to be a master turkey hunter, you must test these tough tom strategies against some of the smartest birds in the woods. What these hunters have learned can save you years of trial and error hunting.

# CHAPTER 7

# BO PITMAN'S OFFBEAT TACTICS

Two kinds of turkey hunters are in the woods -- the ones who call to the birds and require the turkeys to hunt them, and the sportsmen who actually hunt turkeys. Ranking as one of the most tenacious hunters I've ever been afield with is Bo Pitman of White Oak Plantation. Once you know Pitman's background, understanding why he's such a dedicated turkey hunter is easy.

In years past, Pitman rode the bucking bulls in the rodeo. When I asked Pitman why someone with any intelligence would crawl on the back of a wild bucking bull that had both the ability and desire to kill or maim a cowboy, he grinned and said simply, "When you're young, you believe there's nothing in this world -- man or beast -- you can't whip. However, each time you climb on the back of a Brahma bull, you learn in a matter of seconds that there is one critter that can whip you almost any day you get on its back. Something deep-seated in the heart of a cowboy makes him believe he can ride any bull."

This same bulldog-like tenacity which drove Pitman to ride the bulls until his body was banged-up and he had to have pins put in both his shoulders also forces him to hunt wild turkeys. Pitman, who doesn't quit, refuses to believe he can be beaten by a gobbler.

I've hunted in rainstorms, waded creeks, crawled through briars and run with Pitman until my legs have felt like jelly in pursuit of longbeards. I've been with Pitman before when I've been absolutely positive the only reason we were able to bag a gobbler was because the bird just finally gave up. With Pitman, I've sat so still for so long in such a cramped position that when I stood up, I fell on my face because my legs had gone to sleep. But I've laughed with Pitman more than anyone else as I've learned his offbeat ways to hunt gobblers. Once when I was at White Oak for three days, I watched and listened as hunters told me about Pitman's exploits.

"We must have crawled 200 yards on our bellies through a cow pasture," Bob Hickey from Atlanta, Georgia, informed me on the second morning of the hunt as he showed off the fat gobbler Pitman had guided him to take. "Bo climbed up the back side of a tree so he could see the turkeys that were 500 to 600 yards away. I've never seen anyone hunt as hard as Bo."

I asked Bo Pitman to tell me the secrets of his success in hunting turkeys.

## Know A Turkey's Schedule

Because he spends every day of turkey season in the woods chasing gobblers, Pitman has amassed a wealth of turkey knowledge.

"To consistently bag turkeys, the hunter must know where the turkey wants to go, what he wants to do when he gets there and where the hunter should set up to bag the gobbler as the bird goes about his daily chores," Pitman reported. "Each turkey has a set routine that he will follow if he is undisturbed and unpressured.

"In the morning when he wakes up, he will gobble and fly down to meet a hen. Then he'll wander around some -- heading toward where he intends to feed and trying to assemble a flock of hens to go with him. Next the tom will move into his feeding area, feed with his hens, strut, drum, dust and mate until the sun gets too hot for him to remain in an open place. Then he'll enter the shade of the woods to loaf, relax and hang out. About 2:00 in the afternoon, he'll move back to a field where he wants to feed, mate a few more times and perhaps get in a fight. Before dark, that gobbler either will walk or fly out of the field and return to his roost. Once the hunter understands the turkey's schedule and learns where the turkey will be doing this moving around, mating, feeding and loafing, all he has to do is take a stand along the turkey's regular travel route to bag the bird."

Pitman is convinced that one of the biggest mistakes many hunters make is to try and talk a tom into doing something he naturally doesn't want to do--like leave a field and his harem of hens to walk into the woods where he knows danger waits to meet another hen.

*Bo Pitman will do whatever he has to do, including swim rivers, climb trees, and crawl through cow patties, to take his gobbler.*

"Usually you're not going to call a turkey out of a field," Pitman mentioned. "I don't even try to do that. I'd rather wait until the turkey is ready to walk out of the field on his own and then attempt to take him."

## Understand Where A Turkey Wants To Go

"When a turkey is in the field, how can you predict where he wants to walk out of the field?" I asked Pitman who answered, "When a turkey gets too hot to stay in the open, he looks for a place to enter the woods that's clean and where he can see for 30 to 100 yards. That gobbler is not going to pick a spot to go into the woods where there's thick cover and a predator that's been watching him in the field has a chance to sneak up on him."

Then once the turkey starts to make his move, so does Pitman. However, unlike many hunters, Pitman doesn't stand up and run after the turkey but rather belly crawls. Although an average crawl for Pitman may be 1/4 to 1/2 mile, I have known him to crawl further to try to get close to a big, boss gobbler.

"When you're lying on the ground, you can take advantage of bushes and small, low, rolling hills as well as fallen trees to hide your movement," Pitman comments. "A turkey is not nearly as likely to see you when you're flat down on the ground as when you're walking around. Remember, the object of the hunt is to take a turkey. So even though belly crawling may be uncomfortable, that strategy is much more productive than standing up and walking or running, and the turkey's seeing you."

## What To Do After The Easy Way Fails

Although some hunters may say that Pitman's techniques of running, gunning, belly crawling and ambushing a gobbler are not sporting, as Pitman explained, "To get in a position to shoot a turkey when you can't call him is much more difficult than calling a bird to you. The easy way to bag a tom in the spring is to go into the woods before daylight, hear the love-starved longbeard call demanding a sexy hen, make a few seductive yelps and have the ole bird come charging in with sex on his mind and get lead in his head. Anybody can take a turkey like that.

"The crawling and ambushing tactics are what I'm forced to use when the easy way doesn't work. You never will kill some turkeys if you don't ambush them. Understand that a turkey's eyesight is five to 10 times better than man's. Then you'll realize you're stacking the cards in the gobbler's favor anytime you move on him. I'm convinced that outmaneuvering a turkey and bagging him requires much more skill than calling to him. The hunter handicaps himself even more when he has another person with him and tries to let that other person bag the bird."

## Best Times For Ambush Techniques

To bag toms, you must attempt to take the birds when they're on the move before they get to where they're going. Pitman utilizes an appointment schedule for taking gobblers and ranks them according to priority, with the easiest place to bag a turkey being first and the most difficult site or time at the bottom of the list.

"The easiest time to bag a gobbler is in the morning when he flies down off the roost," Pitman emphasizes. "The next easiest time is before he assembles with his hens. If you can intercept the tom before he gets to his feed, you have a fairly good chance of taking him, but your chances are less after the tom has fed.

"If you can catch the turkey coming from his food to his loafing area, you may have an opportunity to bag him. However, more than

*To get in a position to take a shot like this, Bo Pitman wages all-out war on the gobblers.*

likely you're not going to take him in his loafing area. Bagging that bird when he's returning to the spot where he wants to feed from his loafing is almost impossible. But you still have a small chance of taking a turkey if he walks from his feeding site, often a field, into the woods before he flies up to his roost.

"One of the reasons turkeys are so tough to take in their loafing regions is because you can't see them in the woods as well as you can in the fields. Also they don't gobble as much in their loafing areas as they do in the fields. Many times you may walk into a flock of turkeys and spook them if you're trying to hunt them when they're loafing."

## Climb Trees

Since Pitman hunts around many agricultural fields, he may climb a tree 30 to 40 yards off the side of a field to be able to spot gobblers.

*Bo Pitman will crawl on his belly for 1/2 mile to get in a position to bag a turkey.*

"If you're planning to climb a tree to watch turkeys, make sure you climb on the back side of the tree where the turkeys can't see you," Pitman instructs. "Also don't go up the tree if a tom's not more than 150 yards from you. As long as you move slowly and don't climb any higher than you have to be able to see the birds, you can go up a tree and get a much better view of the turkeys and the lay of the land to more accurately make your stalk plans."

Unlike most hunters, Pitman doesn't let turkeys intimidate him. Just as he once believed he could ride any bull he climbed on, he how thinks he can hide from any turkey he can see, whether he's climbing a tree or lying flat on the ground belly crawling.

"I've had birds five to six feet from me that never have seen me when I've been on the ground," Pitman said.

Bob Hickey told me when he hunted with Pitman that Pitman crawled up to the edge of a field and then raised up on his knees to glass some turkeys 200 to 300 yards way.

"As Bo raised up right beside a fence post, I was on the ground 50 yards behind him," Hickey remembered. "Then I heard the beating wings of a gobbler that was very late flying down from the roost. The tom flew right over Bo and landed not more than 50 yards from where Bo was frozen against the fence post.

When the turkey hit the ground, he began to feed. Although the bird stared at Bo, Bo never moved, flinched or blinked. That longbeard looked Bo over good. I don't think the turkey could separate the man from the post since Bo was so tight to the post. Bo held his position for 20 or 30 minutes until the gobbler finally started to feed away from him. Then Bo crouched down and crawled away from the fence post without spooking the gobbler."

68

*Bo Pitman, left, and John Phillips, right, come out of the woods together after an all-day war on gobblers.*

## Be Resourceful When All Else Fails

Every morning during turkey season when Bo Pitman crawls out of bed before daylight and puts his boots on to go chase toms, he resolves mentally that, "I will run as far as I have to run, crawl as long as I have to crawl, climb as high as I must, get wet if necessary and use whatever trick that's legal to help my hunter kill a turkey today."

That kind of determination matched with his own ability to determine what a turkey is going to do makes Bo Pitman a master turkey hunter. Also because Pitman hunts private lands, he's not afraid to try tactics on turkeys that no one else has used.

"Some hunters had come from Pennsylvania to hunt at White Oak," Pitman recalled. "The morning one of them was to hunt, I had an appointment in town at 11:00 A.M. We had found some gobblers in a field, but the birds wouldn't budge. Time began to run out on our hunt. I was desperate. I wanted my hunter to kill one of those gobblers. I knew we had to leave the woods by 10:00 A.M.

"At 9:00 A.M., I decided to use a dirty trick I had played on gobblers only twice before. I pulled off my boots and took off one of my red and white striped socks. I put the smelly sock over my hand and doubled up my fist so my fist looked like the head of a

69

turkey. I laid low on the ground and put that fist out in front of the tree so the turkeys could see it. Next I gave some very aggressive hen calls, moved my sock hand back and forth and then pulled my fake turkey head down. When I peeped out from behind the trees, I saw all three gobblers coming on a dead run. My hunter killed a bird at less than 20 steps.

"I don't advocate utilizing this tactic on public lands, nor do I ever use it except when I'm in the most desperate situation. But on this hunt when time was running out, the sock hand trick produced a bird for my hunter and allowed me to leave the woods on time and make my meeting."

## Learn To Hunt The Toughest Toms

Pitman has learned the toughest gobbler to bag is the bronze baron that keeps all his hens with him all of the time.

"A smart gobbler will keep all his hens out in front of him looking for danger and moving ahead of him," Pitman observed. "Then there's no way a predator or a hunter can take the tom before the hens see the danger. To get this turkey, you must stay very still and let all the hens walk past you. I've even had hens spot me, putt, back up 10 steps and continue to walk down the side of a field to look for another place to enter the woods. Although many hunters will try to jump up quickly to get a shot off at the gobbler before the hens' putting spooks him, I've learned if I'm still, often that tom will continue to walk the same path the hens have taken. Then my hunter can take the bird.

"However, this is the exception rather than the rule. When a gobbler has numbers of hens with him, it's likely a hen will see the hunter, alarm the flock and spook the gobbler. But if that happens, just get to another place to try and take that gobbler or find another tom to hunt before the day is over. Even though I may get beat two or three times in one day by different turkeys, I don't consider the hunt over until I bag a bird, or the turkey flies up to roost. When he's on the roost, he's home free. However, when he's on the ground, I'll stay after him until I get him."

Although some hunters bag an easy gobbler at first light with Pitman, they miss out on turkey war, Pitman-style. When Pitman is on the ground, crawling, low walking, running or just scratching his head trying to determine what a turkey is planning to do, he's ever the master woodsman. To have the opportunity to hunt turkeys with a man like this is equivalent to completing a course for a doctorate degree in the fine art of turkey hunting.

## CHAPTER 8

# HUNTING FIVE TOUGH TOMS

### With Ray Eye

### The Mountaintop Ghost

One of the first gobblers that got me hooked on the sport of turkey hunting and nearly caused me to flunk out of high school during the spring when I was 16 years old was the Mountaintop Ghost. This bird, which gobbled every morning at daylight, lived close to my home on a high ridge. He would gobble from one end of that mountain to the other. But each morning when I climbed the mountain to attempt to get close enough to take a shot, the Mountaintop Ghost hushed and vanished.

After a few mornings of this disappearing act, I wondered if I actually was hearing the bird or was imagining him because I never could see him. I used every tactic I knew, had read about or that anybody suggested to get that tom. I called a lot, I called a little, I set up close to his roost, and I tried to circle him. But nothing I tried put me within eyesight of this ghost-like gobbler, although I missed a few days of school that spring to hunt him.

Finally I learned what the turkey was doing. He'd gobble in the morning and then fly down to a glade where he could see the entire mountain and everything around it. He'd strut there and meet his hens. If he saw me coming, he'd leave.

However, one morning I climbed the mountain before daylight and went to the end of the glade where daily the turkey flew down and walked into that opening. I was 200 yards from where the turkey was roosting when I gave three, soft, tree yelps. The turkey pitched out of the tree, flew to the end of the glade where I was and

71

stuck his head up to look for the hen he had heard in the opening. That morning was when I bagged the Mountaintop Ghost of the high ridge that had forced me to stay out of school and kept me awake many a night dreaming about how I would get him.

This turkey taught me that to take a tough tom, you must learn everything you can-- not only about a turkey but about the habitat where he lives. Once you know what the bird's doing, why he's doing it, where he's going and why he's going there, then the task of taking the gobbler is much easier. Many hunters try to substitute excellent calling skills and wearing camouflage for spending the time required to understand what a turkey wants to do. The Mountaintop Ghost convinced me I had to learn the habits of the turkey first and then worry about how to call him and what camouflage to wear.

## The Baron Of The Black Hills

I met a Merriam's turkey near Rapid City, South Dakota, some years ago and named him the Baron of the Black Hills. This turkey, which always went in the opposite direction when hunters called to him, had a harem of hens for about three weeks before I was introduced to him.

I utilized every tactic I knew. I changed calls, varied my calling spots and even tried to call the hens to me hoping they would bring the gobbler with them. But none of the textbook strategies worked on this bird. After hunting the Baron of the Black Hills for four days, I decided he was just moody. I never could seem to catch him in the right mood to respond to my calling. Another problem I had to deal with was that the turkeys in the Black Hills sounded much closer than they were. So I had spooked a few birds while attempting to get to this tom.

Finally on the fifth day of hunting, I returned to the location where I had been seeing the gobbler with his hens. I waited until the last rays of daylight and watched the turkeys fly up to their roosts. Under the cover of darkness, I crawled into the area where the birds were roosting in the trees. I screamed, hollered and scared all the turkeys off the roost. I carefully watched the biggest bird, which I assumed to be the Baron of the Black Hills, as he flew off in one direction while the hens went off in another direction.

The next morning I returned to the roost site before daylight and walked about 100 yards in the direction where I had seen the big gobbler fly the evening before. At first light, I gave a tree call, but the Baron never responded. Twenty minutes later, I heard

*Ray Eye of Hillsboro, Missouri, the winner of several national, state cnd regional turkey calling championships, has learned his trade as a call manufacturer and professional hunter from the birds he's tried to bag. Eye believes the tougher a turkey is to take, the more the bird will teach the sportsman.*

other turkeys gobbling in the distance. The Baron hadn't even yawned.

I began to give some lost hen calls, which I hoped would fool the gobbler into believing that his hens were trying to regroup close to where they had been scattered the night before. Although the Baron never gobbled, I heard him coming on a dead run straight for me. When the bird was less than 20 steps away, I took this Merriam's, which had 1-5/8-inch spurs. Since that time, I've used this tactic repeatedly to bag boss gobblers that stay with their hens all day and all night and won't respond to calling. The key to success is to separate the gobbler from the hens and then make him try to find his scattered harem.

## The Wheat Field Gobbler

The Wheat Field Gobbler, a Rio Grande turkey, had a reputation near Woodward, Oklahoma, as the turkey nobody could kill. This tom had a flock of hens with him. He could be seen daily when he flew from the woods into an open prairie and then walked out into a wheat field. The Wheat Field Gobbler remained at least 300 yards from the timber. Although he would gobble to almost any kind of calling, no one could budge him out of that field.

*Finally the Mountaintop Ghost stepped into Eye's gunsights, and he was able to take the tom home with him.*

As you know from years of hunting, whenever a new gun comes to town--especially a turkey hunter who has some type of reputation--most locals want him to hunt the toughest bird around town. Turkey hunters are reluctant to give up easy toms that anybody can kill to an outsider. But they love to offer their out-of-state guests the worse turkeys in the county.

Probably there are two reasons for this. The locals hope the out-of-town hunter can teach them a new tactic to take a tough tom and eliminate a problem bird that has had the community upset for several days or even years. Also they want to see if this tom will make a fool out of the out-of-town hunter just like he has the locals. Usually a tough-to-take tom will do just that.

In Oklahoma, I first found out as much information about this turkey as I could. I tried to determine where all the people had set up who had called to him. As I suspected, most of the hunters had called from timbered areas where they could hide.

I decided to go to a fence row out in the middle of the field and stand behind the biggest tree I could find. There wasn't enough cover in that hedgerow to hide a field mouse--much less a hunter. I realized that if I took a stand in front of a tree like I normally would, the bird would be able to see me.

So I knelt down on my knees and laid my gun up against the tree. When the bird came out on the prairie, I gave a few hen calls. The turkey responded but wouldn't come in to where I was. Next, I gave some young gobbler yelps and fighting purrs. Another tom gobbled behind me. Once again I went into fighting purrs and coarse gobbler yelps. This time the Wheat Field Gobbler ran toward me, stopping occasionally to gobble. But before the Wheat

74

Field Gobbler could get to me, he met the second tom I'd heard. Those two birds began to fight about 100 yards in front of me.

When the fight was over, I gave some soft hen calls and a few coarse gobbler yelps to make the Wheat Field Gobbler believe there was another longbeard attempting to move in on one of his hens in the fence row. In 10 minutes, I saw the turkey's fan above a small dip in the hedgerow. The Wheat Field Gobbler walked within 20 steps before I took him. By calling to him from a place where nobody had called to him before, and by creating a situation for a fight after he'd just defeated another gobbler, I caught the Wheat Field Gobbler in an emotional condition that made him come to me. This bird had 1-1/2-inch spurs and was a fine trophy.

## Ralph

However, the Wheat Field Gobbler wasn't nearly as difficult to take as Ralph, a Missouri eastern gobbler that talked and walked. No matter what calls or which tactics you used, Ralph would walk away from you. This turkey left some very good hunters with a severe case of mental depression.

After nine days of our trying to bag Ralph with blackpowder shotguns, my hunting partner, Pat Leonard, and I went after Ralph in the rain. Because Ralph was staying on a ridge, Pat went to one end of the ridge, and I set up on the other end. As Pat clucked and purred, Ralph gobbled but wouldn't come.

Then I set up on a small road just off the edge of the ridge. I had heard Ralph gobbling along this road several mornings in a row. I thought I might have a chance to take Ralph just because I was in a place where Ralph wanted to be.

I clucked four times. Then I put my call down and decided not to call anymore. Pat continued to call. In about 40 minutes, I heard a turkey spitting and drumming nearby. I started spitting and drumming with my voice to make Ralph think another gobbler was in front of him. Ralph gobbled so loud he shook the ground from 40 yards away.

I got my gun up just in time to see the white of Ralph's head as he walked up a little rise. Ralph stopped at less than 20 yards, strutted and stuck his head over the rise to see the other gobbler. That's when I knew I was going to be able to put this bird to rest. I squeezed the trigger on my gun. It misfired. Ralph heard the hammer fall and left the area on a dead run.

Although that was the only time I ever saw Ralph, I did hear him gobble for the next two or three years on that ridge. Many a

*Eugene was a turkey so tough, he whipped all of the men who hunted him, including Eye.*

morning I saw a hunter come down from the ridge where Ralph lived talking to himself. Ralph was a gobbler that just couldn't be killed.

Ralph has helped me learn a very valuable lesson. No matter how good you can call or how much you know about turkeys, sooner or later you will run into a gobbler that can't be killed. No matter how tough you think you are at turkey hunting, one day you'll meet one of these birds like Ralph that will shake your confidence in your turkey hunting ability.

## Eugene

Eugene was another turkey that drove many a turkey hunter to consult with a psychiatrist. Although this bird gobbled from daylight until 10:00 P.M. daily, nobody could get close enough to him for a shot. Eugene was mean. If another tom gobbled in Eugene's territory, Eugene would run at that gobbler, defeat his rival in beak-to-head combat and then return to his home range. I thought about gobbling like a rival and then bagging Eugene when he came in to fight me. But I'm convinced a turkey can tell the difference between a hunter's gobble and a turkey's gobble. Also in most areas, a hunter who gobbles is almost painting a bull's-eye on his head for another hunter to shoot. Gobbling to a turkey is a very dangerous call for a hunter. I don't advise hunters to use it. For three years, I carried hunters from all over the nation with me to try and take Eugene. Because he gobbled so much, the bird always provided an exciting hunt. The people who hunted with me always got to hear the previews but never were fortunate enough to witness the main attraction. I utilized every tactic I'd ever heard of, read about, thought of or could find out. But nothing worked on Eugene.

I believe some turkeys have learned so much from hunters that they just can't be called and killed. Hunters need to know there are birds like this and may have to admit defeat to walk out of the woods with their minds intact. The truly great turkey hunters are the ones who challenge tough birds and take some of them. But they are just as quick to realize there are some turkeys that can't be bagged in this sport that's as much mental as physical.

# CHAPTER 9

# PURSUING HERMIT TURKEYS

### With Allen Jenkins

If you want to be a better than average turkey hunter, learn to hunt hermit turkeys. A hermit turkey ...
... has a PhD in outsmarting hunters,
... is a regal monarch that has survived and has learned from every hunter encounter and
... has faced many combats and deserves to live.

To understand hermit hunting, you first must comprehend what is required for a turkey to become a hermit. In an average clutch of eggs, there may be six or eight male birds. During the summer, predators may take off two. Then in the fall, more accidents may happen, and one or several more birds may die. By the time spring arrives, two or three of those jakes may have survived. Novice hunters probably will harvest one of the remaining jakes. In the fall of the second year, only two, two year old gobblers are left.

Let's say those two year olds survive until after the next spring, and the birds stay together. But during the next season, one of these two turkeys is killed as a three year old. Now there is only one turkey left. All of his brothers have been harvested, and he is the only survivor. Since the gobbler doesn't have a bird to run around with, he becomes a hermit and stays to himself. Rarely will this turkey associate with other turkey flocks-- except with hens during the spring mating season.

The longer the hermit lives, the smarter he becomes, which means hermits are very difficult to bag. Remember that this old, old turkey as a poult has outsmarted owls and coons and later foxes, bobcats and dogs besides other assassins that Mother Nature

*To be able to keep up with a hermit turkey, you need to find a bird with a distinctive track.*

has sent to try and take him. In his later years, he has outwitted hunters by surviving his encounters with man and learning from the hunters' mistakes.

Every second that old tom is alive, he is looking for something to kill him. He knows more about danger in the woods than any other critter. He is the master who has dodged disaster. He never lets down his guard from daylight until dark.

I like to hunt hermits, because I've bagged enough gobblers that just killing a turkey no longer presents the challenge it once did to me. I enjoy the superb challenge of attempting to bag a bird that nobody can take, of trying to hunt the best of the best and of pitting my skills against a world class gobbler. When you reach a certain level of turkey hunting, merely taking a bird no longer is a contest. However, trying to harvest a gobbler that is at least as smart if not smarter than me is true sport.

When there's a gobbler I don't think I can kill, I'll try everything I know to put myself in a position where I can bag that bird. I have used modern tactics like running to get in front of or to circle a hermit, moving closer to a hermit when he won't come in and changing calling positions. But none of the new methods work on hermits for me. Some hermits are so smart that a sportsman may call only twice to the turkey. Then the next time he hears the bird gobble, the bird will be going away from him.

When you locate a hermit, I think that never calling to the tom but instead ambushing him is immoral as well as very unsportsmanlike. By ambushing, I mean if you set up between a field the bird normally goes to, don't call and then try and shoot the gobbler as he walks to that field, then that's like shooting Jesse James in the back. Sure, the turkey is dead-- but what did you prove? You didn't outsmart him, and you didn't outdraw him-- you assassinated him. A turkey that survives to be a hermit deserves a better end than an ambush.

That's not the way I hunt turkeys. I've found that none of the new run-and-gun methods allow me to see the hermit like traditional turkey hunting tactics do. I'm convinced that hunting the old way is the best means for a hermit to be bagged and/or seen. Patience and dedication are the most reliable tools a hunter can employ if he wants to harvest a hermit.

The old way of turkey hunting goes back to a slower time when a quality hunt was more important than how quick you killed the turkey, and outsmarting the tom was the name of the game rather than bagging a gobbler.

Hunting the old way involves ...

... scouting and learning everything you can about a gobbler before you call to that tom,

... taking a stand you believe you can call the turkey to and

... sitting down and trying to call the bird.

Once you sit down to call, the game begins. For you to win, you've got to call well enough to bring that turkey to within gun range. If you can't call the bird to you, the turkey wins, which is how I choose to play the game.

A hermit turkey is sacred to me. I believe he either should be either killed fairly by calling or allowed to die of old age. As far as I'm concerned, when I'm lucky enough to locate a hermit to hunt, then that turkey will die a natural death. Most of the time these old hermits will live to be eight to 10 years old, which is an ancient age for turkeys. Although I've hunted turkeys all my life, I've been fortunate enough to hunt only five or six hermit birds. But these hermits have made the sport of turkey hunting special for me.

## Old Crooked Toe

One of the brainiest turkeys I ever hunted I named Ole Crooked Toe. His middle toe had a crook in it, and I could keep up with his movements by watching his tracks in the mud. When the turkey was three, four and five years old, I could have killed him but chose to let him go so that I could hunt him the following year. Then he could build up his age and the woods sense he needed to become a hermit. I wanted him to get older and smarter so I couldn't kill him.

By the time Ole Crooked Toe was seven years old, he was a master on the subject of hunters and their tactics. I couldn't bag the bird, because he was just too brilliant. He knew every call I made and became so call-shy that each time Ole Crooked Toe heard a hen yelp in the woods, he thought Allen Jenkins was trying to kill him. He got so he wouldn't gobble but about one day a week.

The weather in the spring had to be perfect for Ole Crooked Toe to gobble. He might only gobble five or six times and then hush. Some mornings he might gobble seven to 10 times, but he would stay on the limb and wouldn't fly down for about two hours. I truly believe that when Ole Crooked Toe gobbled, he wouldn't fly out of the tree until he saw a hen. If you called to Ole Crooked Toe, he would fly down the opposite way from where you were calling and sometimes gobble at you going away.

The last time I hunted Ole Crooked Toe, he was between 10 and 11 years old. I hunted him the third week of the season. I heard him gobble that morning. I went to him and set up about 75 yards from where he was roosting.

When daylight came, Ole Crooked Toe gobbled at a redbird. I clucked and yelped softly. He gobbled three or four minutes after I called. I was sure that turkey realized I was the one who had made the call. Although I waited for a solid hour, Ole Crooked Toe

*Ole Crooked Toe, a gobbler Allen Jenkins never did bag, was probably between 10 and 11 years old.*

never gobbled or came to me. When finally Ole Crooked Toe did gobble at a crow, he remained in the tree.

As soon as he gobbled at the crow, I yelped to him again. Ole Crooked Toe flew down out of the tree and gobbled about a half a mile away. Then when he gobbled the next time, he sounded as though he was two miles away. That was the last time I ever heard from Ole Crooked Toe.

One of the most critical factors in developing a hermit and being able to leave a turkey alone long enough for him to become a hermit is having a bird you can identify. If a turkey doesn't have an odd look to him, a certain length of beard, a strange track or some other characteristic that will allow you to identify him, keeping up with that turkey and resisting the temptation to shoot him so you can develop a hermit is hard. I personally would rather hunt a turkey that has a unique track. Then I can track his movements better-- even if I can't see him.

## The Plow Turkey

One hermit turkey I named the Plow Turkey, because the only way I could find him was to plow a specific road he traveled ever now and then. Then I could know if he was still walking up and down that road.

I'd hunt this turkey until about 9:00 A.M. If I didn't hear or spot him, I'd go back home, get the tractor, plow up the road, smooth it down and then return late in the afternoon to locate the turkey's track on that freshly plowed road. If I saw the turkey's track, then I would know he was still in the area. If I didn't observe his track for a day or two, I would wonder if he had left the region. I only hunted the Plow Turkey for about two years. I don't believe that old bird was killed. I think he just finally died.

## The School Bus Gobbler

Another of my favorite hermits to hunt was the School Bus Gobbler, a turkey that roosted within 200 yards of a gravel road. Every morning between 7:15 and 7:20 A. M., a school bus drove down the dirt road close to where the turkey was roosting. When the bus hit the ruts in a certain place on the dirt road, the doors and windows of the bus rattled loudly, and the turkey gobbled in response. But that was the only time the School Bus Gobbler would gobble all day. He wouldn't gobble at logging trucks, cars, motorcycles or anything else going up and down that road.

I hunted the School Bus Gobbler, which was a true hermit, for six or seven years. Although I didn't kill him, I'm responsible for his death, which still makes me feel badly.

I made the mistake of telling too many of my friends about what a challenge the School Bus Gobbler was to hunt. I built him into a legend. I described the areas where he strutted and told everything I knew about the hermit, because I was proud to know that hermit. I got so involved in describing this turkey's strutting regions that some of the other folks I hunted with soon figured out where and at what time the turkey was strutting.

On the opening day of the School Bus Gobbler's 12th season, one of these hunters took a stand in some of the nearby young pines to wait on the hermit. Since I had explained to these people that the School Bus Gobbler strutted for two hours in the early afternoon in these pines and then moved out into the field to feed, this outdoorsman showed up at the pines at about 11:00 A.M.--long before the hermit was scheduled to be there. The hunter made a small blind and waited. He even covered himself with pine straw so that only his head was out from under the straw. When the School Bus Hermit came in to strut, this hunter ended the turkey's life.

After the man realized the evil act he had done in killing the School Bus Hermit, he tried to hide the fact from me and didn't say anything about bagging the bird. But after I hunted the turkey for

84

*A turkey's track may be the last contact you ever have with a hermit gobbler.*

two more days and couldn't find the bird's track, I knew something had happened to him.

When I confronted the man, he admitted to killing the School Bus Hermit. The fellow had tears in his eyes, because he realized how important the School Bus Hermit was to me and how little the turkey had meant to him. The hunter was actually sorry he had killed the School Bus Gobbler.

When I finally learned what had happened, I took a black flowered wreath and tied it to the tree where the old turkey had strutted. That tom had been an adversary, a friend, a teacher and a reason for hunting. Now he was gone. The wreath was a tribute to a noble bird.

We had pitted skills against one another for almost seven years and were friendly combatants. We knew each other very well. The School Bus Hermit understood as much about me as I did him. My feelings were truly hurt when that man went in and ambushed that hermit. I was probably more upset about the that turkey dying than about anything that ever happened to me in the out-of-doors.

When the School Bus Gobbler was alive, I had ...

... called him up often and refused to kill him,

... had the opportunity to shoot him off a limb and didn't do it,

... had the School Bus Gobbler sneak up behind me before,

... met this hermit in the woods many times,

... had many occasions to kill him as a young bird, and

... refused to take him to protect him so he could become the kind of hermit that was challenging to hunt.

The legend was dead, the opportunity to hunt this master turkey was gone, and the bird that had taught me so much never again would be able to teach me. When the hunter informed me he

85

had killed the School Bus Gobbler, I knew I would have to start all over again developing a hermit to hunt. I also realized that two to three years would be required to locate a turkey whose track I could identify, and perhaps three or four years of steady hunting would be needed to train that turkey to become a hermit.

## Why Hunt Hermit Turkeys

If a man wants to learn to be a master turkey hunter, he should find and develop a hermit. A hermit will teach you ...

... patience.

... correct calling, because if you make a bad call, he won't come. You have to learn to sound more like hen turkey than the hen does.

... strategies, including every game a wild turkey can play. When that hermit beats you, you will understand why and put that lesson in your arsenal of tactics.

... quietness in the woods and how to sit still.

You may not get to hunt a hermit turkey more than two or three days each season, because if you put too much pressure on him, he will leave the area. I believe the pinnacle of turkey hunting is for a sportsman to hunt a crafty hermit for several years and have the opportunity to bag the bird but let the turkey walk off so the hermit can die of old age.

## Developing A Hermit

To have hermit turkeys to hunt, the following sequence of events should happen.

1) Find a turkey with an identifiable track.

2) Call that turkey up several times to within killing distance, and then allow him to leave.

3) Realize the second year you try and call a gobbler up after you have let him go two or three times, he will become increasingly difficult to call. You'll have to hunt harder and better just to spot this tom. Run, hide, and use every trick in the book just to see the turkey the third year, because he probably won't answer your calling.

4) Remember the last few years you hunt the hermit that all you may ever see of him is his track. You may hear him gobble from the roost and even strut and drum. But if you can just see that hermit after the first three years, you're a winner. If you ever get a hermit within gun range after you've been fooling with him for about four or five years, you'll know you've become a master turkey hunter.

# CHAPTER 10

# DUELING WITH THE SKULL CLOSET GOBBLER

"I don't know if I can let you hunt the Skull Closet Gobbler," Danny Hawkins of Hawkins Ridge Lodge near Eufaula, Alabama, told me. "The last three men who have gone after the tom have not been heard of since. They just seem to have vanished from the earth. The three sportsmen before them who have hunted the Skull Closet Gobbler now mumble to themselves constantly and haven't been mentally alert since their duels with the turkey.

"This turkey is so dark, he looks black--much like the deeds he performs. The bird reminds me of the Black Knight of old who terrorizes the countryside and then vanishes. Even if we hunt him together, the odds still are in his favor, and our sanity and our skulls may be on the line."

Almost every hunting camp I ever have visited has a resident, legendary, bad gobbler that has defeated every hunter who has hunted him. These birds usually are four years old or older, hunter-wise and lead-shy. These noblest and smartest of the breed throw down their gauntlets to hunters who feel they possess the skill and knowledge to challenge a woods wizard like the Skull Closet Gobbler of Hawkins Ridge.

"This tom's name refers to the fact we believe he collects the skulls of the victims he defeats," Hawkins explained. "Each time a hunter goes after this gobbler, when the turkey gets the best of the hunter we say, 'That ole bird has another skull to take back to his closet and add to his collection.'"

In any sport, the only way to truly test your skill as a competitor is to challenge the best. If you win, you receive the accolades the victor deserves. If you lose, you gain a dose of humility and learn how to win on the next attempt. I always have believed that great hunters challenge great birds.

This Black Knight, known as the Skull Closet Gobbler, had built for himself a reputation that called me to the arena of combat. Although I didn't consider myself one of the greats of turkey hunting, I knew the Skull Closet Gobbler was. He had won this title through right of combat. Hawkins and I would challenge him on his own turf. Win or lose, the Skull Closet Gobbler, Hawkins and I would duel at daylight.

We planned to announce our challenge just before dawn with a soft tree call. Our noble reason for hunting this bird together was because turkey hunting was at its best when shared with a friend. However, the underlying reason was we both believed defeating the smartest turkey in Alabama would take more than one human brain. In the cool morning air of early April, Hawkins and I waited for the Skull Closet Gobbler to declare the contest had begun with his first gobble from the roost.

"He's on that dark ridge about 200 yards away," Hawkins whispered. "When he flies down, he'll head for a small chufa patch to feed up this dirt road. Maybe if we get to the patch ahead of him, we can take his skull home with us."

I've found one trait to be consistent about smart longbeards-- they rarely want to hear very much calling. Most of these older trophy birds that have been hunted hard for several years understand that more than likely a lot of calling is a hunter--not a hen. Perhaps legendary gobblers like this one listen closely for the subtleties in calling that only are produced by the throats of turkey hens.

We took a stand beside the chufa patch and gave a soft tree call consisting of three yelps. The tom gobbled back. We sat quietly for 15 minutes before we heard the turkey gobble on the ground.

"He's coming but to the other side of the field," Hawkins said. "Let's move."

Hawkins and I agreed we had to intercept the Skull Closet Gobbler before he could see the field. This tom had heard what he believed to be a hen in that chufa patch. If he approached this small field and failed to spot the hen while he was still in the woods, the odds were he wouldn't cross the field. We realized older birds that had experienced intense hunting pressure seemed to understand that if they didn't see what they expected to see, they should leave an the area.

*The Skull Closet Gobbler was just smarter than we were. I could see the old bird step into the clearing, strutting and drumming like the proud baron he was.*

We took a stand on the turkey's side of the chufa patch, which enabled us to watch the patch, the dirt road and the woods from where the bird should approach. Ten minutes later, the tom thundered a gobble not 50 yards away. With my three inch Browning on my knee, I readied for the shot that should be presented at any moment.

As the bird moved closer, I could hear him drumming. My eyes burned with nervous perspiration as I anticipated the moment of truth with this legendary bird. We had fooled him. Now I would collect his skull. The mysticism of the legend would be dispelled with the gray smoke from my Browning. After the squeeze of the trigger, and the report of the gun, I would prove this bird indeed was no more than a woodsfowl.

I waited, but the Skull Closet Gobbler failed to offer his head for a shot. Trembling from cramped muscles, I almost jumped out of my camouflage when the bird shook the ground with a gobble not 30 feet away from and immediately behind us.

"He's circled us," Hawkins observed. "He's got us pinned down. If we move, he'll see us. All we can do is sit still, hope he will circle back around us and reach a point where you can take a shot. The bird knows we're here. Now he probably will try to play some kind of devilish trick on us."

Patience is the primary weapon a hunter can use to defeat a hunter-wise gobbler. Remember that most everyone else who has hunted a bird like this has tried to take him quickly.

Twenty minutes later, Hawkins and I heard the Skull Closet Gobbler rattle the timber in front of us again. Hawkins clucked three times softly. The turkey answered. Once more, the gobbler came in and circled around us out of sight but less than 50 yards away behind brush or under the lip of the hill where we were sitting.

"If we can call that bird back in again, I can bag him," I told Hawkins. "Both times the turkey has come to within gun range. But because we've been sitting on the ground and have had cover between us and him, we haven't been able to get off a shot. This time I'll stand up beside this tree. Then I can see him if he comes in range. I have confidence in my camouflage. I'm convinced I can stand still enough so he won't see me. We'll take this ole boy home to dinner."

Hawkins too thought the plan should work. I knew that standing up next to a tree to bag a wily gobbler was a tactic that had produced turkeys for me in the past. The tom gobbled repeatedly as he came to us. Because this turkey loved to talk, he should have been easy to take. However, I realized this assumption was the same one the other noble knights had made who had come to these woods to joust with this Black Knight, who carried a skull and crossbones on his shield and whose black beard protruded out from under his feathered armor. The other knights had been deceived by the ease with which the Skull Closet Gobbler talked. But Hawkins and I would not be fooled.

The longbeard walked in and circled to the right as he had the two previous times. I had picked out a clearing I felt he had to walk through, which was where I planned for him to meet his final challenge. From experience, I was 90- percent sure the turkey would come through that small clearing so I could get off a shot. Between gobbles, I could hear the turkey drum and drag his wing tips through the leaves as he strutted.

Behind me I heard footsteps. Since I knew the Skull Closet Gobbler was in front of me, what could be behind me? The sound of walking in the leaves came closer. Finally I heard the low purring of a turkey hen feeding. Instantly the longbeard gobbled. Immediately the hen began to cut and cackle with fast clucks and yelps.

"We're surrounded," Hawkins reported.

I turned my head away from the clearing and saw the hen standing less than 15 yards from me and looking straight at me. I was camouflaged from head to toe. I even squinted my eyes so the

*Hawkins called, and I stood behind him waiting for the turkey to step out.*

whites wouldn't show. Although the hen knew I was there, she couldn't decide what I was. The longbeard gobbled in the clearing where I had planned to take the shot. But I couldn't move, or else the hen would see me and spook the gobbler. The hen was doing a fine job of calling excitedly. If luck was with us, maybe the hen would call this Black Knight closer to us and perhaps even past us. Then I could get off a shot as they started to walk away from us. But instead, the hen began to slowly drift off to our lefts toward the direction the gobbler was going.

Hawkins, who was better concealed than myself, started giving some excited cutting sounds on his slate call. By sounding like another excited hen, Hawkins had hoped to keep the hen close to us and possibly bring in the longbeard. A hen ready to breed usually would call in most gobblers. The expectation of two ready and willing females we believed would be more than many turkeys could resist--even the Skull Closet Gobbler.

However, this warrior had not gained his sharp spurs and lengthy goatee by letting his desire to mate override his need to survive. The Black Knight walked under the hill where he had been before and strutted and gobbled in defiance to our calling and the pleading of the hen, his lady in waiting. As the bird's masculine yodeling filled my ears, I almost could hear him saying, "I'm the noblest knight in the woods. If you want your offspring to carry my proud, strong genes, you must lower yourself to come to me because here I strut and stand."

When the hen could resist the champion of the woods no longer, she went to him. The two turkeys meandered down the ridge away from us, crossed the bottom and gobbled from the ridge on the next hill.

"I believe the Skull Closet Gobbler sent that hen to check us out," Hawkins said with a big grin. "We had him in gun range three times, and he whipped us all three times. I told you he was a smart and tough bird. Some folks even have started to call him the Gobbler From Hell because he seems to have mystical powers."

I laughed and agreed that this bird seemed to be a very elusive gobbler. But I didn't feel he had performed any supernatural feats so far. He only had been lucky, and the contest wasn't over yet.

We drove to the next ridge where the bird had gobbled. By now, the time was 10:30 A.M. Hawkins and I knew several characteristics about older toms.

Mature gobblers often will breed their hens early in the morning just after they fly down. By 10:00 A.M. or 11:00 A.M., the hens generally will leave the males. Sometimes the gobbler will have a terrific craving for female companionship about lunchtime. Another reason midday hunting is best when you're trying to take older birds is because the heaviest hunting pressure occurs from daylight until about 9:00 A.M. Turkeys that are veterans of several seasons have realized this and understand that danger is present mostly early in the day. They realize few hunters will skip lunch and pursue turkeys around the noon hour.

At 11:00 A.M., the Skull Closet Gobbler reported his position with a gobble that had an eerie, guttural tremble. Without knowing, we had slipped to within 75-yards of the bird. The Black Knight sounded as though he was walking down the same woods road where we were. Hawkins and I quickly sat down near the biggest tree we could find. Before we could call, the sharp-spurred gobbler reported. He was just behind a bend in the road. Surely 10 more steps, and the bird would be in my sight.

We didn't call. We waited. We knew that often relying solely on our knowledge of where a turkey wanted to go and why he

*Back at camp, Danny Hawkins, far right, tells his brother Craig how the Skull Closet Gobbler beat us that morning.*

wanted to go there might result in taking a legendary gobbler. But instead of continuing on down the road, the turkey walked off to our right about 150 yards. Hawkins and I moved parallel to the bird. We were now hunting in 15-year-old planted pines. Because the pines had been thinned, even though the woods appeared to be thick, a turkey could walk comfortably through them.

"We're going to get the Skull Closet Gobbler this time," I told Hawkins. "I'm going to put a sneak on him. I'll crawl 50 yards toward him and sit next to that biggest pine. When I'm set up, give three or four clucks. Then we'll wait him out. Let's sit without calling or moving for at least 1-1/2 hours."

Hawkins agreed this plan should work. If the Black Knight came toward us at all, I should be able to get off a shot.

I belly crawled as slowly and quietly as a church mouse beneath the pews on communion day with a church full of worshipers. Finally I arrived at the tree I had chosen for my ambush and sat quietly. Behind me, I heard Hawkins give three soft yelps on his slate call. Immediately the Merlin of the ridge thundered his noble gobble. The leaves on the pines quivered from the force of the

Black Knight's voice. He was close, very close. I could hear him drumming and strutting in front of me, yet he still was invisible.

I listened as he walked to my right just out of sight. I began to scratch in the leaves with my hand to simulate the sound of a feeding hen, knowing that sometimes when a gobbler was in close, this sound would be the one a hunter needed to make to pull in the bird. The Black Knight gobbled in response to the scratching, and I knew I now had him hooked and on my line. I just needed to reel him in to get a shot. I saw a small, dark body moving off to my right and thought perhaps the Black Knight was a dwarf tom. But as I looked closer, I made out one and then two more small, dark bodies. The Black Knight had sent his pages, three black crows, to scout the woods in front of him as they marched at attention and looked at every tree and bush for danger. The tom gobbled again. My mind began to fantasize that those crows were demon scouts moving out in front of the Skull Closet Gobbler. But then I told myself I'd been hunting too long and listening to too many wild tales about demon gobblers.

As I watched the crows, I glimpsed a patch of white -- the tom's head -- just behind the three black birds. When the white vanished behind a bush, I adjusted my position, mounted my shotgun and prepared for the showdown with this demon of the South Alabama hills. The longbeard gobbled. My heart almost skipped. I saw the Skull Closet Gobbler in full strut--tail fanned, head coiled like a striking rattlesnake, and all his feathers erect as they reflected the rays of the sun.

I decided to let the tom come out of the strut and cross the clearing. I told myself I had plenty of time. I waited on him to force him to give me a good shot.

The Black Knight seemed to float across the clearing in full strut. He broke his strut and stepped into my side of the woods not 30 yards away. My finger tightened on the trigger as I silently pushed the safety off and said a prayer. As I concentrated on the shot, I saw a sapling about the size of a half dollar directly between the turkey's neck and head and me.

"I can make the shot," I told myself. "I mustn't rush it. All the bird has to do is take one step, and I'll have a clean shot. He doesn't even have to take a step. If he just leans forward, I can shoot."

However, the bird never moved. He simply rolled his eyes, looked straight at me and recognized my human form. The Black Knight putted, squatted and ran off -- never offering a shot. As the Skull Closet Gobbler trotted off into immortality, I spotted what seemed to be a bulge under his left wing. Looking closer, I almost could swear I saw my own head being carried away.

# CHAPTER 11

# SCOPING TURKEYS

I am totally convinced after a year's worth of research that adding a scope to your shotgun greatly will increase your odds for bagging a turkey. I've hunted with and without a scope for several seasons, and the turkeys I've missed are the ones I've taken a shot at without the advantage of a scope on my shotgun.

Three, longbearded gobblers were coming straight at me one day last spring. Each bird's goatee was at least eight to 10 inches long and was full and thick like a rope.

The first bird I put the bead of my shotgun on would have weighed better than 19 pounds and would have been a fine prize by any turkey hunter's standards. The second tom was strutting. Because of his age, size and superiority, he demonstrated his dominance, while the other two gobblers, the one behind him and the one in front of him, cowed in his presence. Of course I wanted to take the big bird--the strutting gobbler that claimed the right to breed the hens. I let the first turkey pass and took aim at the wattles on the strutting bird. When I squeezed the trigger, instead of seeing a tom tumble and flop, I watched as the big turkey gathered air under his wings, flexed his muscles and climbed for the sky.

I didn't take the second shot because I couldn't believe the first shot had missed. Although I was convinced I couldn't have missed, I had. I had the sickening feeling in my stomach that accompanied failing to take a turkey I'd spent hours hunting and calling.

## Why We Miss

I began to investigate why we miss turkeys to solve my own problem. One of the reasons we all miss turkeys is because our shotguns may not pattern shells properly. Often a gun will deposit the largest number of shot either above, below or to the left or the right of the turkey's head.

In the past to correct this patterning problem, you had to compensate by aiming either high, low or to the left or the right of the target rather than aiming right at the spot where you wanted the most pellets to hit. Even though a gun that patterned best a little off-center of the target might down a gobbler, you could not deliver the maximum density of shot as you could if the shotgun shot straighter. If the turkey moved his head slightly as you squeezed the trigger, or if the gobbler was standing in some brush or cover, the gun might not deliver enough pellets into the kill zone to bring the bird down.

Another reason you miss is because you don't get your cheek down on your stock. When a longbearded gobbler walks into view, you may bring your shotgun to your shoulder, concentrate your vision on the turkey's head, see the bead on your shotgun and fire. However, because your cheek is not on your stock, you are not aiming properly and will miss your turkey.

The turkey's head is relatively small, about the size of a woman's fist, which is difficult for even the most proficient shooter to hit. At 30 yards, the target appears very small. Also in most areas of the nation, the wild turkey gobbler is a bird of shadow and shade. Although a turkey will move into fields and pastures, most often when you hunt him, the bird will be in some type of woodlot or cover.

Many believe the best time to hunt turkeys is early in the morning just at first light when the birds fly down. Because of low light conditions, spotting that white head often will be difficult and seeing the wattles you want to aim at can be impossible. If the turkey's head is brighter, perhaps many of us will be able to aim better, shoot straighter and miss fewer birds.

Yet another reason we may go home with an empty game bag during turkey season, even after we squeeze the trigger, is we misjudge distance. Turkeys often appear to be much larger than they are. Often you may assume a bird is at 20 yards or less when the tom is standing at 40 yards or more.

Although some shotguns will deliver fairly dense patterns at distances more than 30 yards, and some successful turkey hunters shoot turkeys at more than 30 yards, I try never to take a shot at a distance greater than 30 yards. I believe my chances of bagging a

*A scope on your turkey gun allows you to have a brighter, larger target.*

bird are at least 50 percent greater when I remain under that 30-yard range than they are if I exceed that distance when I take a shot.

Several years ago I had climbed to the top of a steep mountain and had a big Merriam's gobbler less than 20 yards from me in a clear field. All I had to do to down the bird was to lean and shoot around a small pine tree about 10 yards in front of me. When I leaned to my right and bent from the waist to take the shot, I missed the turkey completely. After chasing the bird unsuccessfully, I returned to the tree I'd been sitting up against and went through the motions that had been required to take the shot.

"There's your problem, John," a friend of mine, Dale Faust, said. "You're canting your shotgun."

## How To Scope A Shotgun

Because I believed a scope could remedy many of the problems I had discovered that caused me to miss turkeys, I had to decide how to mount the scope of my shotgun and which type of scope would be best for turkey hunting. I wanted to put the scope on my Remington Model 1100 SP three inch magnum, because this gun was tried and true and one of my favorite turkey guns. However, the idea of drilling and tapping this gun for a scope made me queasy. If using a scope for turkeys proved to be a bad idea, I didn't want to have those ugly holes in my receiver. I searched for an alternative.

I found a unique mount, the B-Square produced by the B-Square Company. Not only did this mount require no gunsmithing to attach to the shotgun's receiver, but it also was idiot-proof. All I had to do was remove the pins from the receiver and replace them with the pins for the mount. This mount could be put on and taken off without changing or damaging the receiver in any way. If a scope for a turkey gun proved not to be a good idea, I could remove the mount. No one ever would know I had tried this idea.

I used Weaver rings and chose a Nikon 1.5-4.5X20 variable scope, which was very bright and clear and had a 67.8-foot field of view. I wanted low power because most turkeys I planned to shoot would be at 30 yards or less. I knew a quality scope like the Nikon 1.5-4.5X20 with its large exit pupil and maximum light transmission would cause objects to be brighter and clearer than they appeared to the naked eye in low light situations. The whole system looked impressive. But until I began to fire the gun, I didn't learn the true value of this system for hunting turkeys.

## How To Pattern With A Scope

When I took my scoped shotgun to a shooting range, I shot at a turkey's head target with Winchester Premium No.6 shot. Although the gun and the shells performed admirably, and the pattern that both produced would have downed a bird, the largest part of the shot pattern was below and slightly to the right of the wattles on the turkey head target. I fired a second shot just to be sure that the pattern was consistent, and it was.

By using the windage (left to right) and elevation (up and down) adjustments on the scope, I was able to move the cross-shaped reticle. Then the next time I shot and aimed straight at the wattles, the shot was delivered in exactly the right spot with the densest pattern on the turkey's neck and head, the area I wanted to cover. Now I would not have to compensate when I aimed to get the best pattern on the turkey's head. I also noticed when I brought the shotgun to my shoulder that the eyepiece of the scope was at precisely the correct place for my eye without my having to lower my cheek on the stock, because the B-Square mount was higher than the bead on my shotgun.

This information means that when your scoped shotgun comes to your shoulder, you don't have to remember to get your cheek down on the stock to aim properly or depend on your reflexes. The scope is at the best spot for you to see and shoot without lowering your head. This advantage is especially helpful when you have to take a quick shot and forget to put your cheek on the stock.

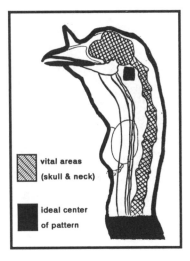

vital areas
(skull & neck)

ideal center
of pattern

*A turkey head target like this can let you
see where your pattern is the most dense.*

The size of the target also is magnified by the scope. Because the target appears larger, you can aim much more accurately. Even if you move slightly, you still can keep the crosshairs in the center of the target. However, one disadvantage that can be associated with enlarging the target is that inexperienced hunters may think a gobbler is closer than he actually is.

When I kept the scope on 1.5X, I was able to see the end of my gun barrel. I quickly noticed I had a tendency to cant the gun to the left. This problem was one I never realized I had before I put the scope on the shotgun. I was able to discover this flaw in my shooting because when I held the gun straight, the vertical portion of the reticle would be off to the right of the bead of my shotgun, as I looked through the scope. When I straightened the gun, I shot more accurately and eliminated my canting problem. From this experience, I learned that when I saw a turkey's head in my scope, besides looking at the reticle, I had to check how straight I was holding the gun by observing where the vertical line of the reticle intersected the bead on the end of my barrel.

## On-The-Field Performance

Any system of hunting can look good on paper or sound good when you discuss it with a friend. However, the acid test is when you take your theories and your guns into the woods to hunt.

I was somewhat nervous the first day I carried my scoped shotgun to hunt a turkey. I didn't know how much of a factor my

*In the woods, the scope comes to the eye more easily and quickly than your having to get down on the stock to shoot.*

using a scope, which could result in losing a portion of my peripheral vision, would figure in the ultimate outcome of my hunt.

I also was concerned about the amount of abuse the Nikon scope and the B-Square mount could take. I might fall off a bank, wade through a swamp, have to climb a mountain or accidentally bang my gun into the side of a tree when I was hunting. I knew the bead on my shotgun could handle all my misadventures, but I wasn't certain the finely-tuned sighting system I now had on my shotgun could weather the storm of a hunt with me.

"Do you think that scope will work?" Danny Hawkins, one of the owners of Hawkins Ridge Hunting Lodge near Eufaula, Alabama, asked me.

Hawkins, an avid turkey hunter, was a good friend who knew we'd both be disappointed if we spent the morning finding, calling and waiting on a turkey to appear and then missed the bird because my idea of utilizing a scope on a shotgun for turkey hunting proved to be less than satisfactory.

"I think my idea will work," I told Hawkins with an air of confidence I really didn't have. I was trying to assure myself more than Hawkins. "I've tested it on the range and the pattern board. If I'm right, we can have a better gun for hunting turkeys."

Just before first light, we heard a turkey gobble. We had to walk down a clearcut, wade a small stream and climb a steep hill to get to a site to call to the bird. Each time the gun bumped a tree or was jolted, I was like an expectant mother carrying her firstborn.

Finally, we set up on top of a ridge in a cleared-off area and called to the tom. The gobbler answered. Fifteen or 20 minutes

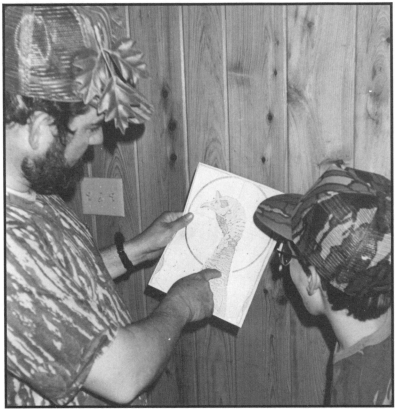

*The scope on the turkey gun can help you put the densest part of your pattern in the kill zone of the turkey's head.*

passed before I saw a cotton-colored head snaking through the grass about 1-1/2 feet off the ground. The tom was coming in silent. Because of our calling, the turkey expected to spot a hen in that clearing. He was reluctant to leave the woods without seeing the hen.

However, Hawkins did some low, coaxing calls. The bird responded by walking through the fresh dew of early morning. The turkey came in quickly and stopped at about 25 yards from us before I could get my gun up. Since the tom was looking straight at us, there was no way to move, shoot or call. All we could do was pray that our Trebark camo would prevent the gobbler from seeing us. The turkey stood and looked at us for what seemed to be hours but was actually only about eight to 10 minutes.

"Take him when you can," Hawkins whispered.

Any move I made would spook the bird. Finally the turkey turned to walk away from us. When he did, I mounted my shotgun quickly. The crosshairs found the base of the gobbler's head as the turkey moved away. I squeezed the trigger. The bird tumbled.

Although I was excited about taking the turkey, I was more excited my theory had worked. My fears of not being able to see the crosshairs quickly and easily and being able to sight in on a moving target as accurately as I could with the bead on the shotgun proved to be unfounded. I couldn't have asked for a better performance from the gun or the scope than they both had produced on their first outing. But one hunt was not enough to convince me that a scoped shotgun was a better way to hunt turkeys.

A few weeks later I was hunting with Cecil Carder of Fort Worth, Texas, on the McPherson 4M Ranch near Sonora, Texas. The size of the Rio Grande turkeys in this area was legendary. These birds offered another opportunity to test the wisdom of putting a scope on my shotgun during turkey season.

Carder and I hunted hard all day long. Although we called up several jakes, the longbeards eluded us. Just before dark, we saw a big gobbler strutting on the edge of the field with a harem of hens. We circled the field and got behind the gobbler and his hens. We set up to call. But because the old bird had plenty of feminine company, we didn't believe our calling would cause him to walk away from his steady dates to check out the new girl on the block.

Finally just before fly-up time, the hens began to move toward us but never saw us since we were concealed in Mossy Oak Greenleaf camouflage. They walked within less than eight feet of where we sat motionless praying for the old gobbler to come out of the field and present a shot. The woods were dark. Since we were shaded by some plum bushes, I realized that sighting would be very difficult. However, I could hear the gobbler drumming less than 30 yards away. I knew in a short time I'd be presented with a shot.

I rested my Remington on my knee and tried to keep my pencil from jumping out of my breast pocket as my heart pounded. Then I spotted the huge tom in full strut, less than 25 yards away. I looked through my scope and was surprised at how clear and bright the gobbler's head appeared. I realized immediately I could see much better with my scope than I could if I had been relying on the shotgun's bead. The tom came out of the strut, took one step forward and placed his wattles at the intersection of the two crosshairs on my scope. I bagged the bird.

# CHAPTER 12

# BOWHUNTING TOMS
# THE MAXIMUM TEST

Nerves of steel, the confidence in your shooting to challenge the legendary Robin Hood, the woodsmanship of Daniel Boone and the positive attitude of Dale Carnegie are all characteristics required to bag a gobbler with a bow. Most bowhunters agree that going after gobblers with a bow usually means the odds are 10 to one against you. For every 10 times you encounter a tom within bow range, you only may take that bird home on one of those attempts. Some of the best turkey hunters and bowmen in the nation will tell us why.

## David Hale

"When you hunt turkeys with a gun, you must be very conscious of your movement so you don't spook the bird," David Hale, one of the owners of Knight & Hale Game Calls and a leading turkey hunter with either gun or bow, said. "As a bowhunter, you have to be doubly conscious of not giving away your position when you attempt to draw your bow or move your bow to take the shot."

According to Hale, a bowhunter must be much closer to a turkey than a gunman when he takes his shot.

"The shotgun hunter can bag a bird at distances up to 40 yards without too much trouble. But the bowhunter needs his gobbler at 20 yards or less to have the best opportunity to inflict a lethal shot.

"When a gobbler is that close, you must have a way to hide your movement of drawing the bow. I carry a portable blind I can kneel behind and shoot over or through, or I look for some type of bush I can hide behind. The hunter who uses a shotgun can sit in front of a tree and doesn't have to worry too much about back cover, because he blends into the tree trunk."

Hale, who shoots a mechanical release, prefers to utilize camo paint on his hands and face rather than wearing camo gloves when he's hunting turkeys.

"I don't want anything between my finger and the trigger of the release," Hale explained. "If you wear a glove and shoot a release, oftentimes the glove will make you shoot before you're ready to take the shot. To prevent that from happening, I prefer to wear camo paint."

Hale also likes to kneel instead of stand when he takes a gobbler.

"When I'm hunting turkeys, I want to be on the same plane with the tom and be able to see what he sees," Hale commented. "You'd be surprised how much more you can see when your eyes are on the same level as the turkey's eyes and how much different things look from a kneeling position instead of a standing position."

Although many outdoorsmen set their bows up differently when hunting gobblers than they do when hunting deer or other big game, Hale does not. Hale does not want to relearn how to shoot his bow for turkeys. Because Hale is confident in the way he shoots, and the accuracy he has, he believes the bowhunter who consistently shoots accurately should not do anything to influence that accuracy.

When Hale is ready to draw the bow, he's tried to pick a place in the woods where the turkey will have to step behind a bush or some type of brush to give him those few seconds required to make the draw. Once Hale is at full draw, he favors a shot at the turkey's back.

"Since the spine shot, in my opinion, is the best shot you can make on a turkey, if the bird is going away from me or has his back to me, I'll have the opportunity to shoot for the spine," Hale reported. "If the turkey is in strut, I'll shoot for the spot where the wings join the body--again hoping to get a spine shot. If you shoot into the turkey's breast, more than likely you'll loose the bird. If the turkey has his tail fanned in a strut with his back to me, I shoot for the spot where the tail feathers join the body."

Hales prefers a Rocky Mountain III broadhead and does not use an arrow stopper.

"I don't change up my arrow or my bow in any way when I'm hunting turkeys," Hale advised. "I believe I can be just as effective in harvesting a gobbler without an arrow stopper as I am with an

*To get in close enough to take a turkey with a bow, the hunter must remain motionless until he's ready to shoot.*

arrow stopper. The most critical key to equipment is to have a bow that delivers the arrow quickly and shoots a flat trajectory. Your accuracy in shooting is much more critical to your success than whether or not the arrow stays in the bird."

Sometimes Hale employs a unique strategy for bagging toms that matches the skill and expertise of the hunter to the turkey hunting situation. Then the odds are more evenly stacked in the hunter's favor.

"If I'm hunting with a good bowman who's never hunted or called turkeys very much, I like to use a three man team to get the novice turkey hunter a shot," Hale said. "We'll set a Feather Flex turkey decoy in front of the blind to get the bird's attention. The archer concentrates on his equipment and making the shot. The second man in the blind tells the bowman what the turkey is doing and what the bowman should be doing to get in position to take the shot at the turkey without spooking the bird. The third hunter, the caller, is 10 to 20 yards behind the blind calling to the turkey and trying to work the bird in front of the archer. By using this technique, an archer without much hunting experience can go into the woods and have a fairly good chance at success in taking a tom with a bow."

Often Hale recommends that sportsmen form a two man team, which includes a bowhunter with turkey hunting experience and a caller who will manipulate the bird.

"On a two man team, the archer has at least hunted turkeys before with a gun, knows what a turkey probably will do and realizes when to draw and shoot," Hale explained. "This bowman can focus all of his attention on the turkey and not have to divide his attention by attempting to decide when to draw the bow, concentrating on the turkey, trying to call and knowing when to take the shot."

The ultimate challenge is when a bowhunter goes one-on-one with a turkey.

"To go one-on-one with turkeys, you must be a proficient caller and be able to work a bird into you with a diaphragm mouth call," Hale advised. "You also should have had some turkey hunting experience to realize when to move and when not to move on a tom. Also you have to be an excellent archer to shoot straight and take the proper shot."

Using these three hunting systems, you can match your turkey hunting knowledge and archery skills to the task of taking a bird.

## Dale Faust

Dale Faust of Liberty, Mississippi, who has won 3-D silhouette shoots, field archery competition and just about every award the Mississippi Archery Association has to offer, agrees with Hale that, "The best shot to take at a turkey is the spine shot. Because turkeys will not leave a blood trail like deer and other big game animals, you may have a difficult time retrieving the turkey, unless you break the bird down."

Faust believes a bowhunter should shoot as heavy a poundage bow as he can draw smoothly and hold comfortably for an extended time.

106

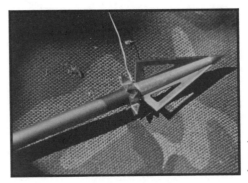

*An arrow stopper like this one can help deliver more of a punch for the bowman.*

"If you have to strain to draw the bow back, you'll move more than if you draw smoothly," Faust suggested. "Then the turkey will spot you. If you're trying to hold a bow that's too heavy, you may have to let down on the bow just a second before you're ready to shoot the bird. One of the keys to bagging a longbeard with a bow is to be as comfortable and relaxed as you can through the draw and during the time you have to hold the bow.

"I shoot a 72-pound PSE and a Land Shark broadhead made by Simmons, a broadhead that's about 160 grains and has a 1-9/16-inch cutting radius. Although I put a star type stopper behind the broadhead, I don't use the stopper with the intention of stopping the arrow in the bird. I use the stopper for extra drag and knock-down power. I've found when hunting turkeys that to be successful you must use bigger broadheads that inflict more damage on impact. The large broadhead will go through more parts of the turkey and is more likely to cut vital areas than a small broadhead will."

Faust is convinced one of the key mistakes many archers make if they get a good hit on a turkey is chasing the bird. He thinks you're more likely to recover the gobbler if you wait for 10 to 15 minutes after you take the shot.

"Another mistake many hunters make that I've made in the past, is to have too much blind," Faust advised. "Before I've built blinds and then have been unable to get a shot at a bird when the turkey has walked up within bow range. I've become more concerned about back cover and trying to use less cover in front of me. Then if I do get a bird within range, I can move the bow to a spot where I can draw and shoot. If you have sufficient background cover, and you've camouflaged yourself and your equipment properly, you may be able to let that turkey walk past you and get a good shot at his back. Sometimes I've found that wearing camouflage clothing and paint may be more important than using a blind to hide the hunter."

Although David Hale relies solely on a mouth diaphragm call to work a gobbler in close when bowhunting for turkeys, Faust uses a combination of calls.

"Primarily I use a Lynch box call or a slate to initially call a turkey," Faust explained. "When a turkey is in bow range, the bird should be looking for the hen, and I shouldn't have to call him. When a turkey is within 30 yards, I don't want to be thinking about anything except what the bird is doing, when I'm going to draw, and where I'm going to place the arrow. I don't need to use my boxes or slates then. However, I've never found that using box calls and slates has inhibited my ability to call a turkey within bow range. I do keep a diaphragm call in my mouth. If the turkey turns his back to me just out of bow range, I may want to purr or cluck a few times--just to let the gobbler know where I am. But I do my serious calling with my friction calls."

When Faust is aiming at a turkey that is quartering away from him, he doesn't shoot for where the wings enter the body like most hunters do. Instead, he aims just above where the drumsticks go into the bird's body, because, "That's where the vital area is, and the region where you most effectively can get a quick kill. Many times if you're shooting down on a gobbler and you hit the point of the wings, the arrow will go through the breast rather than through the vitals. That's why I use the drumsticks of the bird to point the way to the area I want to sight in on."

When Faust is ready to shoot, he'll often wiggle his elbow or move his bow slightly since, "A turkey usually will stop and turn sideways just before he leaves an area if he sees movement. The two seconds or so that elapse from the time the turkey spots me and presents the shot before he leaves is the critical time to release the arrow to get a good hit.

"The hunter's making some type of small movement is especially effective when the turkey is in the strut. A bird spotting that movement generally will drop his strut, stick his neck straight up and present a stately, erect shot for about two seconds. Knowing ahead of time a tom will do this, already being at full draw and finding the spot you want to hit quickly will enable you to release the arrow in time to take the gobbler."

Faust is a believer in hunting in twos when attacking longbeards.

"I only want to be six feet away from the bowman hunting with me, if I'm calling the bird," Faust reported. "I want the turkey to

*A blind increases your chances of taking a turkey.*

know where I am and come straight to me. Then the archer can get the shot."

Unlike Hale, Faust shoots with fingers and a tab, but he cuts the fingers out of his glove so the tab will fit properly, and he can feel the string.

"I put camo paint on the tops of my fingers, paint my arrow rest, color my wheels and my cables with a black marker and use dull-colored nocks and dull-colored fletchings on my arrows," Faust said. "Then nothing about my bow or me that the turkey can see will cause him to become suspicious."

Faust never picks up his bow until he's prepared to take the shot. Instead he leaves the bow resting against a small tree or a bush with an arrow nocked and an arrow holder keeping his shaft on the arrow rest.

"Then when I see a turkey coming, I pick up my bow and get ready for the shot," Faust commented. "My arms and hands are not fatigued, and I can draw easier and shoot straighter."

Faust also has learned the value of using decoys in the states where they are legal.

"A turkey decoy will keep the turkey's attention focused on the decoy instead of the hunter," Faust mentioned. "Also sometimes a gobbler will come in to that decoy and walk around it. When the longbeard has his attention focused on that decoy and starts to circle it, he'll often present that back shot for which I'm looking."

# Brad Harris

Brad Harris, Public Relations Director for Lohman Calls, has been hunting turkeys with a bow for 15 years. Harris shoots a 75-pound Hoyt Pro Force Extreme. Some archers consider this bow to be too much weight for hunting turkeys.

Harris explains. "I use the same bow and the same setup for hunting elk and deer as I do for hunting turkeys. I'm more comfortable shooting off my knees, which is how I position myself when hunting turkeys with this bow at this weight, than I would be if I had to change the weight of the bow or use another bow.

"Because turkey hunting can be very intense by its very nature, I feel I have to be as comfortable as possible in my stand and with the equipment I'm shooting to shoot accurately. But I do believe that because turkeys aren't a dense animal a hunter can be just as effective with a 50 or 55 pound bow as he can be shooting one as heavy as mine."

For a broadhead, Harris prefers the Satellite Titan because, "This larger broadhead will give me an extra cutting edge. Also the Titan is four-bladed and cuts a good-sized hole. However, which broadhead you shoot is not as critical as correct arrow placement when you're trying to take a turkey with a bow."

Harris, who has mixed emotions about string trackers, allows the terrain and the distance of the shot he must take to dictate whether or not he will utilize one.

"For shots less than 20 yards in open areas, the string tracker works well," Harris explained. "However, I've found on shots more than 20 yards away, I lose some accuracy with a string tracker. I also feel the arrow is inhibited if you're hunting in brushy terrain and using a string tracker, because the string often will become entangled in the brush through which you're attempting to shoot. I shoot without a string tracker most of the time. However, I have bagged gobblers when using a string tracker."

Harris, like Hale, does not advocate the use of arrow stoppers to stop the shaft in the bird and possibly inflict more damage because the arrow is staying in the bird and continuing to cut as the turkey moves.

"Shot placement is the most critical part of the hunt," Harris reported. "If you put the broadhead into the turkey where it should go, you won't have need of a string tracker or any type of arrow stopping device."

Harris doesn't advocate utilizing a blind either but rather prefers to move unencumbered to the gobbler he's calling.

*Brad Harris of Neosho, Missouri, PR Director for Lohman's Calls, and longtime, avid turkey hunter, uses his calling skills to get turkeys in close enough to take them with a bow.*

"I try to call numbers of turkeys in a day and work with several turkeys to get them into position so I can take a shot," Harris said. "Because I cover a vast expanse of ground to work numbers of turkeys, I don't want to carry gear like a portable blind around with me. I run, gun and work as many turkeys as I possibly can in a day.

"Turkey hunting with a bow is a numbers game. The more turkeys you can call to you, the better your odds are for bagging one of them with a bow. The only time I do use a blind is when I'm trying to make a video of bowhunting a bird. Then I'll find where a gobbler is strutting, feeding and watering, set up a blind and decide to sit there until the turkey shows up. But I feel using a blind is much less efficient when you're bowhunting."

To prevent the turkey from seeing him when he's calling or drawing, Harris tries to find two large trees relatively close together.

"I use one tree for back cover and have the other tree right in front of me," Harris mentioned. "I can hide behind the tree that is in front of me and make my draw. The tree behind me will help to conceal my movement from anything approaching from the rear."

Harris also uses turkey decoys at times but only in certain hunting situations.

"If I'm hunting around a field or in open timber where the turkey can see a long distance, I'll set up a decoy to distract the gobbler," Harris advised. "But when I'm hunting in dense cover where the turkeys will not be able to see for more than 30 yards, I don't use a decoy. When I can see the turkey, I should be at full draw and waiting for the turkey to present the shot."

If Harris is hunting alone, he uses a diaphragm mouth call exclusively. However, when he's calling for another bowhunter, and they're team hunting toms, he may utilize a wide variety of calls including boxes and slates.

"An effective way I've been involved in bagging turkeys with a bow is to put the archer 30 to 40 yards in front of the caller," Harris said. "Then as the turkey comes in, the caller changes positions to manipulate the turkey to the spot where the archer can take a shot.

"For instance, if the gobbler is coming in to the bowman's right, the caller will move to the bowman's left and begin to call to attempt to turn the turkey and make him walk in front of the archer. The caller always keeps the shooter between himself and the turkey and tries to pull that gobbler right over the shooter. Using this tactic, all the archer has to do is concentrate on the shot and the turkey. When the turkey gets close to the bowman, the caller should call very aggressively to get the turkey to double-gobble and triple-gobble. Then the bird will be so excited the archer will have an opportunity to draw his bow and make the shot."

Harris prefers aiming at the point of the wing forward to the top of the tom's head.

"Although I miss quite a few birds shooting this high, when I do connect with a gobbler, I generally break the turkey's neck or spine and don't have to run through the woods chasing after him."

Like Hale and Faust, Harris thinks the best shot is when the turkey is quartering away from you and looking away from you. Then you can get a shot at his back.

These three master turkey callers, hunters and bowmen have given tips to simplify the task of trying to take a tom with a broadhead. However, always remember you'll miss more gobblers than you'll bag when hunting turkeys with a bow. But with each miss and every mistake, you'll be inching closer to success.

# CHAPTER 13

# SMOKING GOBBLERS WITH BLACK POWDER

Years ago, anyone hunting with black powder knew that after the smoke cleared, he would either have a delicious, tasty dinner that night or would fall asleep to the sounds of his rumbling belly growling and cursing the lack of food. Our ancestors in frontier times were not interested in the sport of turkey hunting. When they raised their muzzleloading shotguns and settled the beads on the heads of gobblers, taking food was their primary consideration. Therefore, the art of hunting turkeys in the old days was very important.

Two of the fastest growing sports in America today are blackpowder hunting and turkey hunting. The sheer numbers of turkeys available to hunt are increasing rapidly as are the numbers of those who are taking up the sport. Also, a natural evolution occurs in turkey hunters who are successful with conventional weapons and then seek a more challenging way to bag the longbeards of spring by hunting with black powder. To smoke a gobbler with black powder today, you must employ many of the skills of the early settlers.

## Solving Blackpowder Problems

"The turkey hunter puts limitations on himself when he picks up a blackpowder gun to try to bag a bird," Dick Kirby of Orchard Park, New York, explains. "Taking a turkey with black powder is much more challenging because the gun may misfire. Also you don't have the range with a blackpowder shotgun you do with a three inch magnum 12-gauge shotgun or a 10-gauge shotgun, which means a gobbler must be closer to you if you're to bag him.

"To get a turkey closer, you'll have to be much more patient, and your calling must be more subtle. With a smokepole, you generally only get one shot, unless you're shooting a double barrel. Too, you must be prepared to deal with the bird's possibly detecting the sound of the gun's hammer being cocked and then being spooked."

To overcome these problems, Kirby offers the following suggestions. "To prevent misfires, after I've shot two or three caps through the nipple to dry out the barrel, I then load the gun and pour a few grains of powder in the nipple hole. Next, I screw the nipple back in, which puts powder close to the cap and eliminates most of the problems of misfiring."

According to Kirby, most conventional three inch magnum 12-gauges or even 10-gauges can take turkeys effectively from 35 to 40 yards. But with a blackpowder shotgun like the CVA Trapper, Kirby prefers to have his bird at 30 yards or less. One of the advantages to the Trapper shotgun is the screw-in choke system.

"By using the full choke, the gun will hold a tighter pattern over a greater distance and place more pellets in the kill zone of the turkey than a shotgun that doesn't have a choke," Kirby reported.

To test the patterning of our blackpowder guns with and without the chokes, we fired the guns at 32 steps, shooting 1-1/4 ounces of both shot and black powder at a turkey head target. We counted the holes in the target and found the gun had put 12 pellets in the kill zone of the neck and head. Next we removed the choke, loaded the gun the same way and watched as the pattern began to lay down from 15 yards to the target with only two to three pellets being delivered to the kill zone. Kirby and I determined that to consistently bag gobblers with a blackpowder shotgun, some type of choke system was a must.

"One of the true joys of hunting turkeys with black powder is having to wait to get the birds in close," Kirby mentioned. "If you'll let the turkey come in as close as he will before you shoot, you'll be able to notice many things about turkeys you may not learn when you take turkeys at long range.

"You can watch the bird flip his snood out of the way to look more closely for the hen. You'll also learn that when a bird is in close, many times he'll stick his neck up very suddenly and crane it as though he is looking for a hen. Even though you think the gobbler is preparing to putt and run off, if you'll wait, most of the

114

*Dick Kirby of Orchard Park, New York, president of Quaker Boy Calls and expert turkey hunter and caller, has learned to fine tune his turkey hunting and his blackpowder skills. He uses his Boat Paddle box call to lure the bird in close enough to take him with black powder.*

time, you'll see him lower his head, come in closer and then crane his head again and continue to look for the hen."

## Setting Up

Wil Primos, President of Primos Game Calls, believes that since black powder often shoots slower than conventional powder and sometimes a blackpowder gun may not shoot as tight a pattern as a conventional shotgun will, then how you set up to take a turkey is critical to your success.

"With a conventional shotgun when some grass or a few twigs are between you and the turkey, and you don't have a clean shot, the power of your shot can clear out the underbrush, and you can bag the turkey," Primos mentions. "However, with a blackpowder shotgun, I don't believe the shot is as forgiving as with a conventional shotgun.

*Wil Primos, president of Primos Game Calls who enjoys hunting toms with conventional guns, black powder and bows, gets most excited when he bags turkeys with black powder.*

"When I hear a tom gobble and start going to the bird, I hunt slower, study the terrain more and am much more selective about my choice of the place I'm going to call the turkey to than I am when I'm hunting with a conventional shotgun. I even have had to back up on a turkey before to attempt to pull the bird into a clean area to take the shot with a blackpowder gun.

"When I have a blackpowder shotgun in my hand, my hunt is much more intense. I have more to think about and more mistakes to try and overcome, and I tend to hunt slower and more cautiously than I do when I'm holding my three inch magnum. I'm convinced that blackpowder hunting is much more challenging and more exciting than modern hunting for turkeys. I like having to check and recheck my equipment and my hunting tactics. Also I get to pit my skills as a woodsman against a tom."

## Learning The Smoke Pole

Bob Hickey, President of Connecticut Valley Arms (CVA), has become a turkey hunting enthusiast with black powder in the last several years.

"I've always enjoyed the sport of blackpowder hunting," Hickey commented. "However, turkey hunting with a blackpowder shotgun is one of the greatest hunting sports in which I've ever participated."

*Bob Hickey believes no challenge is greater than taking a tom with a blackpowder gun.*

Although many of the frontiersmen bagged birds with muzzleloading rifles, today those who hunt with black powder generally prefer a shotgun. The blackpowder guns available for the turkey hunter give you two options -- either a single barrel or a double barrel.

"Many hunters prefer the double barrel because it gives them two shots at a gobbler," Hickey reports. "Oftentimes that second shot is critical to bringing a bird down. Our CVA double barrel has two improved cylinders. Besides being an excellent turkey shotgun, this particular weapon is also suitable for firing a 60-caliber patched roundball for deer hunting. With the double barrel shotgun, you have both a roundball gun (a blackpowder gun for hunting deer) and a scatter gun (a blackpowder gun for hunting turkeys).

"The other shotgun offered by CVA is the Trapper shotgun, which combines the best of both worlds since it is a percussion cap blackpowder shotgun which allows you to hunt the old way, plus the gun comes with screw-in chokes, which gives you the option of hunting with improved, modified or full choke. This gun has swivels for a sling and a recoil pad on the stock. If you can't get a gobbler to within that 20 to 25 yard range that the improved cylinder barrel offers, than you can use the full choke and reach out a little further to bag your gobbler."

## Deciding On The Charge

On all muzzleloading shotguns, you have the option of either using Pyrodex, a synthetic propellant, or the more traditional black powder.

"If you're going to use Pyrodex, RS-rifle powder is recommended," Hickey advised. "If you're shooting blackpowder, use FF black powder. On all blackpowder shotguns, you should load by volume with equal volumes of shot and powder."

Using a volume metric measure, a light load is considered one ounce of shot and one ounce of powder. The maximum recommended by most companies is 1-1/4 ounces each of shot and powder.

Although most of you who hunt turkeys with black powder will want the heaviest load possible to get more powder and shot to the bird, if you've never shot a blackpowder shotgun before, you'll soon learn that these guns can rattle your fillings loose when you begin to take the recoil. Since you'll have to pattern the gun and then be required to shoot that gun at a turkey, you may prefer to shoot either the one ounce or the 1-1/8-ounce load rather than the maximum load. Even if you can handle the recoil, when you shoot a heavier load, and you expect the gun to kick, you may flinch at the shot and pull the gun off the turkey. Many experts feel that shooting a lighter load that will not cause you to flinch will insure your accuracy better than shooting the maximum load.

"To get the best results, pattern the shotgun first with a one ounce load and then begin using the heavier loads if you choose to," Hickey advises. "The heavier loads will give you a denser pattern at a greater distance than the lighter loads will."

Two different systems are utilized for loading blackpowder shotguns. The one piece plastic wad system, which consists of a 12-gauge plastic wadding cup that can be bought at any hardware store, is rammed down the barrel and over the powder. Once this

*By eliminating the problems associated with blackpowder hunting, you can bag a bird each season with this primitive weapon.*

plastic wadding shotcup is in place, the pellets are poured in, and a paper overshot wadding is rammed down over the top of the shot. Easy and quick, this system doesn't require you to carry as much stuff in your pockets as with other types of loading.

The independent wad system includes an over-the-powder wad, which is a disk of very, very firm cardboard about one inch in circumference. You pour the shot in and then add a paper overshot wad.

I prefer the one piece plastic wad system for several reasons. The plastic wad usually has a cushion between the powder and the shot, which acts as a shock absorber and reduces the shock from the powder to the shot before the shot leaves the barrel. This cushioning of the initial blast helps to reduce the amount of shot deformity that occurs when the charge goes off, and the pellets are compressed against one another. A deformed shot doesn't fly straight, and the pattern tends to open out more than if the pellets remain round. The plastic cup also prevents the shot from hitting the sides of the barrel of the gun as the shot exits the gun, which aids you in shooting a tighter pattern.

"I believe that No. 6 shot size is as small as the turkey hunter should consider," Hickey reports. "If he's shooting a full choke gun, he even may be able to shoot No. 5s or No. 4s -- depending on how the gun patterns."

119

The good news about shooting a blackpowder shotgun for turkeys is you can experiment with loads using a mixture of No. 4s and No. 6s to see how they pattern at various ranges. You can custom build a load just for your gun and the amount of powder you want to shoot and the range at which you wish to shoot. When you hunt with a blackpowder shotgun, every element of the hunt becomes much more personal and more customized.

## Calling The Blackpowder Gobbler

Dick Kirby believes that when you are hunting with a smokepole, you need to know more about turkey calling than you do when you are hunting with a conventional shotgun.

"Most hunters call too much and call too loud," Kirby observes. "But to be effective in taking a turkey in close, you need to decrease the volume and the amount of calling as the bird comes to you. The closer the turkey comes, the less you should call."

Kirby calls turkeys like he plays cards. He eliminates a call from his hand once he plays it.

"I never give away my best calls until I absolutely have to bring in the turkey," Kirby commented. "When I start dealing out calls to the gobbler, I'll give him some cutting calls and cackling calls to get him excited and make him gobble. These calls often will drive a tom into a frenzy. Sometimes he'll come to you, however, often he'll walk away from you. Hens will do this type of excited calls in the spring but rarely. Therefore, use these calls sparingly.

"Then once you've dealt these calls, which initiate conversation with a turkey, eliminate them from your calling arsenal. When the tom starts to talk to you, give more subtle calls, softer calls - lighter yelps and softer clucks. The key to getting a gobbler to come in close is changing your calling so you're not calling to the turkey to locate him, but rather he is calling to you to learn your position. Be aware of when the conversation changes when you're bringing a turkey in from your trying to determine his location by calling to when the gobbler is attempting to find you by calling and walking toward you. Then you'll be able to bring the bird in very close to get that 30-yard or less shot."

## Getting Comfortable And Becoming Invisible

Another key to taking a turkey with a smokepole is to sit still and wait on a good shot. Although many hunters think when they hear a turkey gobble close by that the bird is going to be in front of them in five to 10 minutes, this happens only rarely. Most of the

*The key to getting a gobbler to come in close is changing your calling so you're not calling to the turkey to locate him, but rather he is calling to you to learn your position.*

time, you will have to wait from 20 minutes to possibly two hours to bring in that bird. Being comfortable on your stand for a long time so you don't have to move or if you do move, having that movement be unnoticed is a critical factor for success.

Being camouflaged from head to toe is particularly important when a turkey is 30 yards or less from you when you're hunting with blackpowder. Kirby chooses the Trebark II camo pattern, because he feels the colors blend in well with the woods he hunts.

"I also use a headnet with the wire around the face opening, which allows me to formfit the eye and nose area around my glasses," Kirby says. "The first thing you look for when you set up is an area with a tree you can lean up against and enough ground cover in front of you to let you use a friction call like the Boat Paddle, a box call, or some type of slate or glass call without being seen. I like a cushion to sit on to add more comfort to the long wait. I never sit on my leg because it will go to sleep.

"If and when you have to move to get more comfortable, survey the region around you slowly 180 degrees to make sure you can't see a turkey. Then wait on some type of sound to cover your movement. Generally I move when a gust of wind blows, an airplane passes overhead, a train whistle sounds, or an 18-wheeler rolls by on a nearby interstate."

Utilizing an effective insect repellent like Johnson & Johnson's Deep Woods Off or Wisconsin Pharmacal's Repel or Repel with Earth Scent are other ways to keep a hunter from moving. Then you won't be tempted to swat a mosquito or scratch a tick or a redbug. However, remember even the best insect repellents will lose their potency if you're hunting in hot, humid weather, and your perspiration causes them to be diluted. I carry a can of spray repellent in my game bag and apply it frequently during the hunt to the most critical areas - my hands, head and ankles. Even though the bugs may not be able to get through headnets and gloves, often the sounds mosquitoes make can trigger an instinctive swat reaction which can and will spook a gobbler.

Another factor that causes turkey hunters to spook birds when they're in close is having to sneeze, cough, clear their throats or wipe their eyes -- indicative of sinus problems usually associated with spring woods heavy with pollen. Before I leave in the early mornings to hunt turkeys, I take an antihistamine which won't make me sleepy like Tylenol Sinus to alleviate these problems.

## Knowing When To Take The Shot

"Besides the requirements of sitting still and being quiet to be successful on turkeys, with a blackpowder shotgun you only have one shot most of the time, even if you're shooting a double barrel," Kirby advised. "Don't rush the shot. Take your time, sight down the barrel, and see the target clearly before you squeeze the trigger.

"The best way to make sure the bird is in range is to predetermine the distance of 30 yards before you see the bird. Decide not to take the shot unless the turkey is within that 30-yard killing zone. Once the gobbler comes into that area, hold your shot, and watch his head. The gobbler has 270-degree peripheral vision, and his head zips around like a periscope. When you see a turkey's head, don't move because he will spot you. If he observes you, he will leave, and you won't get the shot."

## Cocking The Hammer

When the turkey is coming in, and you're preparing for the shot, you have to make the decision of when to cock the hammer. Most hunters will carry their guns at half-cock when hunting. When you begin to call to the turkey and the gobbler answers, look at the nipple on your shotgun and make sure the percussion cap hasn't fallen off. If it has, replace it. If not, you have to determine whether to cock the gun and wait on the bird with a cocked gun

*Blackpower hunters feel a kinship with the early frontiersmen and pioneers after a successful hunt for gobblers.*

ready to shoot, or when you're ready to squeeze the trigger, cock the gun and hope the resulting click doesn't spook the turkey.

"Often the amount of hunting pressure the turkeys have had will help you determine when to cock the hammer," Wil Primos suggested. "If the turkeys haven't been hunted much, when you cock the hammer, the gobbler may stick up his head to see what has made that sound. Then you'll have a clean shot at the turkey's head and neck area. If the turkeys have been hunted intensively, and they hear that click, they may leave the area before you get your thumb off the hammer."

"Personally, I believe waiting until you're ready to take the shot and then cocking the hammer is safer," Bob Hickey commented. "Even if you spook the gobbler, you shouldn't sit for an extended time with your hammer back, and the gun loaded."

If you ...

... like to custom build your loads,

... enjoy the challenge of having to get closer to a turkey to bag him and

... want to feel kinship with the early frontiersmen and pioneers, then you'll enjoy holding a rabbit-eared double barrel gun, listening to a gobbling turkey walking through the leaves and remembering the stories your grandfather has told of how his grandfather once hunted.

CHAPTER 14

# WINNING AT THE MOMENT OF TRUTH

The turkey behind me screamed his gobble. The hot blast of air on the back of my neck I thought I could feel each time the bird reported made the hairs on my neck and arms stand at attention. The tom was very close--less than 10 yards away.

I knew I could take the gobbler. All I had to do was roll over on my side and aim quickly. Then the longbeard I'd been trying to call for over 2-1/2 hours would be mine. "Gobble, Gobble, Gobble, Gobble, Gobble."

I quickly rolled to my side. But before I could get the gun to my shoulder, the turkey was gone. I watched as a black spot disappeared behind a large water oak before I ever sighted in on the bead on my shotgun.

In those early days of my turkey hunting so many years ago, I learned the lesson most veterans already know that even if you're the quickest gun in the West, you can't outdraw a gobbler in his own living room. Most of the time, when a hunter doesn't bag his bird, he has failed to act properly at the moment of truth. Like the bullfighter who stares death in the face and only has his knowledge and his skill with a sword to make him either a hero or a goat in the arena, the turkey hunter faces that same moment of truth when a gobbler is in close, and he has to make a decision of when, how and where to take the shot.

Here's a look at several different moments of truth that you surely will be faced with if you hunt the longbeards of spring for many seasons.

## The Gobbler Is Behind You

Patience is the most important virtue a turkey hunter can exercise when trying to take a longbeard. Your patience will be put to the supreme test when you have that turkey you've been working all morning appear less than 20 yards behind you gobbling his head off.

The first tendency you have to fight is to sneak a peek. In this situation, the turkey's so close that more than likely you will spook him--if you move even the slightest to try and see the bird. This tom's looking for a hen. If he spots any movement that's not a hen turkey, his danger alarm will go off, and his feet will take wings. Instead, sit still, and don't move.

The best action to take is no action. The turkey either will do one of two things--walk around in front of you or walk off. Either move the turkey makes will allow you an opportunity to bag him. If the turkey walks in front of you, don't try and take him when he's six to 12-steps from you unless he steps behind a tree or a bush where he can't see you or turns his back to you. Make the final adjustments with your gun before taking the shot. Then wait on the shot to be presented.

If the turkey walks away from you, and you believe he's out of sight and can't see you, look at your watch. Wait another 15-minutes. Then move around the tree to face in the direction where the turkey has gone and try and call him back to you. If the turkey won't return to your stand, change calling sites and calls when you're sure he won't spot you. Then begin to call to him again.

## Your Gun Is Down And The Turkey Is Coming

One of the worst situations to get caught in when turkey hunting is to have your gun in your lap and the turkey moving straight to you without a chance of bringing your gun to your shoulder without the bird's seeing you. You may be able to quick draw on the turkey. If you move quickly and start to bring your gun up, many times the turkey will stop and stick his head up to look around because he is surprised. Then you will have time to take the shot. But this tactic has a low percentage of success. Usually the turkey will be able to see you move and get away from you before you can get off the shot.

A more productive technique is to let the gobbler keep coming and pray he'll stop, begin to strut and turn his back to you or step behind a tree before you have to make a shot. If not, then let the

*I learned early in my turkey hunting career that you can't outdraw a gobbler. Even if you get your gun up quickly, the bird will get away.*

turkey pass by you. Don't try and take the shot. Either attempt to call him back to you, or change calling sites and call to him again.

Once again, patience will be your best ally. Often a hunter fails at the moment of truth when turkey hunting because he rushes his shots and tries to take the shot before the turkey presents a shot. Ninety percent of the time when you force a shot a gobbler doesn't give you, you'll miss the bird.

## Gobblers That Are Henned Up

With 13 pairs of eyes looking for you, making a successful shot at times almost can be impossible. I found myself in this situation when I hunted in Mississippi with a friend of mine, Dale Faust. We had called a gobbler with hens into a small hardwood bottom where we'd been hunting all morning.

Earlier in the morning, I'd seen three gobblers and bagged one in this same spot. The other two gobblers had walked to their strutting area about 150 yards away on a ridgetop. Twelve hens had gone to the gobblers just after daylight. We continued to call to the birds. After two hours of calling, the hens finally came to us, and we could see one gobbler walking behind them in full strut.

127

"Don't even blink your eyes, John," Faust said. "If we can let the hens walk past us, I believe I can get a shot at the gobbler."

Some of the hens came as close as eight feet from our stand. I squinted my eyes so they wouldn't see the whites and stared so I wouldn't blink. But as Faust had predicted, the hens walked past us. Then he took the gobbler at 30 yards. We bagged two gobblers from the same stand on the same morning using this tactic.

When a gobbler is with hens, you have to be as conscious of the hens as you are of the tom. The hens constantly are looking for danger. Many hunters will concentrate so hard on taking a shot at gobblers, they forget the hens may see them move when they make their final adjustments for their shots. Only when you know for certain the hens can't spot you should you try and take a shot at a tom.

Even if the hens and the gobblers pass you, often you may be able to call the gobbler back to you by giving some light clucking and purring and by scratching gently in the leaves. When a tom hears soft hen talk, he may return to you--believing one of the hens has strayed out of his flock and that he needs to return and herd her into his harem.

Even if they get past you without shooting, you may be able to remain in that same place, take a nap and call that same gobbler back to where you are after the hens have left him later in the morning.

## You're Under A Gobbler

Often I've located a turkey gobbling from the roost late in the afternoon or in the early evening. Then I've known that all I have to do to bag that turkey the following morning is to get within 100 yards of where he is roosting, let him gobble from the roost and give some light tree calls and a fly-down cackle just at daylight.

Although this easy, traditional way will bag a spring gobbler, one of the mistakes I've made in the past is to get into the woods before daylight, sit down and wait for the turkey to gobble. Then when the longbeard finally does wake up and begin to talk, he's perched on a limb not 10 feet from where I'm sitting.

The best strategy is to do nothing. If you call, the gobbler will expect to see a hen close to him. If you move even the slightest, the bird will spot you. Wait and see what happens. When the turkey flies out of the tree, he'll either fly close to you or away from you. If he lands close to you and steps behind a tree or a bush, you may have the opportunity to prepare for and take a shot.

128

*One of the worst things that can happen to a turkey hunter is to have a tom walk up behind him.*

If he flies away from you, you still have an excellent chance of bagging this gobbler. Wait two minutes by your watch, and then begin to give some cutting, cackling and loud yelping calls. You want to make this tom think you're a hen that's responding to his calling from the roost. Now you've shown up for the date, and he's not at home. The calls should sound like you're agitated and demanding him to come and mate with you as he's promised when he's gobbled from the roost. Often this tactic will bring a gobbler running back to you. Once more, patience pays off.

## The Hung-Up Gobbler

When a turkey is standing 40 to 50 yards in front of you at the end of your gun barrel screaming his gobbles, a war goes on in your brain. Your dark side says, "I can force the shot and probably take the turkey." The light side says, "The turkey is too far away. If you try and take a shot, you're either going to injure the bird and not be able to recover him, you're going to scare him off and not be able to hunt him anymore, or the turkey will beat you fair and square. He will win the day, and your hunt will be over." Two alternatives you can use to still win the day and bag the bird without having to force the shot are to let the bird walk off, move closer to him and try and call him back or to circle the turkey, get out in front of him,

*What you do when the gobbler is standing in front of you often determines whether you win or lose the game of turkey hunting.*

change calls and attempt to call him to you. But a better option maybe to put your hand in the leaves. Begin to scratch like a hen when the bird's not looking -- particularly if the turkey can't see you all the time. Scratch with a cadence of scratch, scratch, pause, scratch-- which is the sound a hen turkey makes.

If the turkey is just over a ridge and I know he can't see me, I'll often have a stick three or four feet long beside me when I sit down. I'll move that stick back and forth in the leaves to simulate turkeys walking. Or I'll take my hand and press it on the leaves to try and simulate two steps being made by a heavy bird. Turkeys expect to hear more sounds from a hen than just her calling. If a gobbler comes in and hangs up, he needs to hear other, reassuring sounds that will let him know a hen is just out of view. If you can think like a turkey and use the sounds a turkey makes other than calling, many times you can bring a hung-up gobbler to within gun range.

## When To Take The Shot

If the bullfighter plants his sword either too quickly or too late when the bull charges, he may find himself on the horns of the bull or suspended in the air between heaven and earth after the bull hits him. For the turkey hunter, if he shoots too quickly, he'll often miss the bird. Or, if he waits too late to shoot, the gobbler often will get away from him.

How do you know when to shoot? Here's two rules of thumb. When the turkey steps within the 30-yard perimeter I've set up in my mind before he arrives to take him in and presents the first good

130

*Brad Harris has learned how to avoid misses and often takes a turkey home for dinner.*

shot, I shoot rather than letting him move any closer. Or, if I want to see how close I can allow a tom to come before I take a shot, I continue to aim until the bird sticks his neck up and putts, which means he is alarmed. If you don't take the shot when the gobbler putts, he will be gone, and you probably won't get a shot.

However, for every rule in turkey hunting, there are plenty of toms that break the rules. Sometimes even when a turkey doesn't break the rules, you still may miss.

Brad Harris, an avid turkey hunter, utilizes 10 tactics to prevent missing turkeys at the moment of truth.

## Ten Tactics To Prevent Misses

"1. Have confidence in your shooting ability. To know what will happen when you squeeze the trigger on your shotgun, pattern your gun at distances of 10 to 40 yards before you go into the woods to hunt. Once you understand how the gun patterns at varying distances, then you'll have the confidence you need in your equipment to down a tom when he is within range.

2. Learn to judge distance accurately. If you're not sure how far a turkey is from you in the woods, then you don't know whether he is in the range of your shotgun or not. Estimating distances you

are from an object in the woods and then stepping off that distance will help you learn to judge distance more effectively.

3. Concentrate not only on the turkey as he approaches but also on the bead of your shotgun. You must be able to see that bead as well as the turkey to shoot accurately. Often a turkey hunter who watches a gobbler move within range never sees the bead on his shotgun when he pulls the trigger.

4. Know where to place the shot. If you aim for the turkey's head and neck, you'll bring the bird down much more efficiently. By aiming at the gobbler's wattles, the largest part of your pattern usually will cover the kill zone.

5. Have patience. Oftentimes you'll miss a turkey because you try to rush a shot and take it too quickly. Wait on the turkey to present a good, clean shot, or else don't shoot.

6. Sit in a comfortable shooting position. If you're not comfortable, and you can't sit motionless for an extended time, you may begin to fidget or shake as your muscles cramp, perhaps just as you take the shot. Then you may miss.

7. Position your gun where you can take the shot. If you shoot right-handed, quarter slightly to the right. You want to face slightly to the right of the turkey you've called into where you are. Then you'll have at least 180 degrees you can turn and get off a shot. If you're a left-handed shooter, quarter slightly to your left for the same reason. Never sit facing straightaway to a turkey.

8. Use a quality insect repellent. If you have a tick crawling up your leg, a mosquito buzzing in your ear or a deerfly stinging, you'll find concentrating on the shot difficult. Insect repellent keep bugs from biting you and insects from distracting you when you're trying to take a turkey.

9. Develop confidence in your calling skills. If you know you can call a wild turkey, then you won't be nervous when you have to make calls, and the bird is in close. If you don't believe you can call a turkey, this lack of confidence may cause you to miss the bird when he is in close.

10. Wear camouflage you're convinced works the best at hiding you in the area where you hunt. If you're covered up with camouflage clothing from head to toe, and you know the turkey can't see you, then you won't be as afraid to move when you must. You'll also be willing to let a bird get in close enough for you to take a good shot without feeling you have to rush the shot before the turkey spots you."

# CHAPTER 15

# LESSONS FROM GRAYBEARD GOBBLER CHASERS

As I topped the mountain after crawling over 200 yards of blown-down trees in upstate New York, my heart was pounding, my breathing was labored, and my camo clothing was as wet as if I'd been in a swimming pool. Being 20 pounds overweight and 46 years old, I asked the question sooner or later we all must, "How long will I be able to turkey hunt?" Then I began to remember some of the graybeards of the sport like 90-year-old J. R. Eubanks of Atlanta, Georgia, who told me he planned to quit turkey hunting when he was 102, which was the age he'd set for retiring from his business where he still worked five days a week.

"Uncle Roy" Moorer was 93 when I hunted with him in Evergreen, Alabama, a few years ago and was one of the best woodsmen I ever had met. Although Uncle Roy wouldn't win a 100-yard dash, if there was a contest for walking around the world, my money would have been on Uncle Roy.

Older turkey hunters may not be fleet of foot, but they consistently take more turkeys each year than the younger, more aggressive hunters do. These men all have logged more years of hunting than I am old. From the number of birds they've brought in each season that they have taken or that they have called up for other hunters to bag, I've realized their brains contain mountains of turkey hunting knowledge.

We in the turkey hunting fraternity all tend to listen to and try to pattern ourselves after the celebrities in our sport. But if you really want to know how to consistently bag more gobblers every

*When Uncle Roy Moorer of Evergreen, Alabama, was alive, he was one of the greatest turkey hunters who ever lived.*

spring, listen to the masters who have logged the most springs of turkey hunting. Not only can we learn from their wisdom, we can take heart in the fact that they have proven we can go to the sound of Meleagris gallopavo every spring well after most of our friends only listen to the squeaking of their rocking chairs.

Harry P. Bibbus, of Moundville, Pennsylvania, has been hunting wild turkeys for 43 years and, at 77 years old, is still going strong.

"The longer you live, the more you learn about turkeys and turkey hunting, and the more you enjoy the sport," Bibbus explains. "Fourteen years ago, I had my left foot amputated. I do more sneaking up on gobblers than hurrying up on gobblers now. I believe that by going slower, I don't scare off as many turkeys as the fellows do who hurry to get to the birds. I know since I'm older I can sit and wait on a turkey much longer than in my younger days. Today I may wait several hours on a turkey, although a younger hunter may get up and leave a turkey before the bird reaches him."

Bibbus, like most veteran turkey hunters, has learned when you've got a call that consistently produces turkeys year after year, there's no reason to change calls.

"I have a small cedar box with a slate top that I use with a striker to call turkeys," Bibbus reports. "Although I made the box

134

*One of the best ways to kill a really tough turkey is to keep notes on him, according to one old timer.*

back in the early 40s, it still calls turkeys just as effectively today as when I first built it. But I also use a diaphragm call. I don't do anything fancy with my calls. I just try to call to the tom the same way he calls to me to give him some encouragement."

*Clyde Jackson of Red Bay, Alabama, has an entire room dedicated to his turkey hunting. Jackson says he wakes up at 3:30 A.M. year round, just hoping turkey season has arrived.*

Bibbus believes one of the reasons an older hunter often will take more turkeys than a younger hunter is because of his age and experience in the woods.

"I learn something from every turkey I hunt," Bibbus mentions. "I just about know where a turkey wants to go before the turkey knows."

Bibbus is a student of the wild turkey and calculates and predicts where a turkey may be and when he should be there with topo maps, aerial photos and his log.

"I keep notes in a log on every hunt I've ever made-- even back to the late 40s," Bibbus comments. "One of the best ways to kill a really tough turkey is to keep notes on him. Every time you hunt

*Most graybeards of the sport of turkey hunting take great pride in teaching young hunters the masters' secrets.*

him, write down what you've learned about the bird, where he travels and when he travels. Before long, you can study your notes and determine what that gobbler will do because of what he's done in the past. Having a blueprint of that turkey does not mean you can take him but just that you are putting the odds more in your favor. Studying turkeys with my notebook and my maps allows me to hunt turkeys when I'm not actually in the woods. Although I don't hunt every day of the season, I hunt more days than I stay at home."

Bibbus, a fall as well as a spring turkey hunter, has found that bagging a longbeard in the fall is one of the greatest challenges of turkey hunting.

"Because I'm older, much more patient, willing to wait on a gobbler in the fall and to study my maps and notes when I'm not hunting, I may have an advantage over a younger hunter who is not willing to spend the time required to harvest a longbeard fall gobbler."

When I wondered aloud how much longer Bibbus would be able to turkey hunt, he answered, "I'm in good health now. I believe I'm good for at least another 10 years of serious turkey hunting."

J.R. Eubanks, who has been hunting turkeys for more than 50 years, comments. "In the 40s, not too many turkeys were in Georgia. But in recent years, so many birds are present to hunt that the only way I can keep the game sporting is to not shoot unless I can get two gobblers in close enough to take them both with one shot. In Georgia, we're allowed two turkeys per season. Usually I hunt until I'm able to get two turkeys with one shot, and then my season is over. If I only succeed in getting one turkey with a shot, I generally won't hunt anymore. For two years in a row, I've taken two gobblers with one shot."

Eubanks, who is from the old school, believes that once a turkey is coming to you, you don't need to continue to call.

"I use my old M. L. Lynch box that Mr. Lynch made and signed for me about 40 years ago," Eubanks recalls. "All I do is give a few yelps. When I know a turkey is coming to me, I rarely call again. I just wait the bird out. Most older hunters will give a gobbler a chance to do his own thing and come in naturally rather than calling so much and trying to force the bird to move.

"Something else I've learned is to remain motionless without moving. Although I've always been able to sit fairly still when I've been hunting, now that I'm older, I can stay still longer. Movement by the hunter spooks a turkey more often than anything else. Younger hunters tend to move more than older hunters do. If a turkey's coming to you, the longer you can sit still, the greater your chances will be for killing a turkey."

Today, Eubanks dresses in Mossy Oak camouflage and utilizes an umbrella type blind. But in the old days, Eubanks remembers that, "When we didn't have camouflage, I just wore the same hunting clothes I used for quail hunting and deer hunting. I made sure I had my face and hands covered and that I leaned back against a big tree. Taking a turkey back then was the same as today.

"If you'll stay absolutely still when a turkey approaches, more than likely, he's not going to see you. But if you move or fidget the slightest, he'll be gone. I think the main reason older hunters are much more effective at taking turkeys than many of the younger hunters is we don't have to hurry up and do anything. We've learned that one of the main secrets for success in life and in turkey hunting is patience. I believe patience is more responsible for a turkey hunter being successful than all the calling and camouflage there is in the world today.

*From the graybeards, we've learned you rarely get too old to hunt turkeys.*

"A patient turkey hunter will get a chance at some time during the season to take two toms at one time--if he spends enough time hunting to get two gobblers with their heads close enough together. I took two in one shot in 1988, two in one shot in 1989 and would have taken two in one shot in 1990. I had three gobblers coming into my blind. I waited until two of the bird's heads were close enough so there should have been enough shot to kill both--if I shot between them. But when I shot, both turkeys ran away.

"I couldn't understand why I hadn't taken both of those birds with one shot. No.6s should have spread enough to kill both those birds. When I looked at my empty shell, I saw that I had No.2 shot instead of No.6 shot. That's why the pattern wasn't wide enough to take either turkey.

"I've promised myself and some other folks that I will retire at 102. I still work every day and hunt turkeys every spring."

Clyde Jackson of Red Bay, Alabama, 76 years old, took his first turkey in 1949. Last turkey season he hunted almost every day of turkey season. In the 1990 season, Jackson and his son limited out on gobblers, but in 1991, he said he had a better season because, "Even though I didn't take as many birds, I broke in three new turkey hunters and helped them each kill their first turkey the first time they went hunting. I had much rather help new hunters bag their first birds than take a gobbler myself."

Jackson believes he's a better hunter now than when he was a younger man because he can hunt much more relaxed.

"If a longbearded tom outsmarts me, he's won that day in the woods," Jackson comments. "I don't get upset and want to kick my dog or hit something like a younger fellow may. If a turkey wins, he wins. If I win, that's okay too. But win, lose or draw, a turkey doesn't get me as upset emotionally as I think he does younger hunters.

"However, I can't take anything away from the younger hunters. They have much more information today to learn how to turkey hunt than I did when I first started. The equipment is much better also. When I first began turkey hunting, if I wanted a turkey call, I had to make my own. Also then there were no magazines or books to read on turkey hunting, and few people you could talk to about turkey hunting.

"Hunters today also have better guns than I had when I first started hunting, even though the guns are more expensive. I think next year I'm going to put either a peep sight or a scope on my turkey gun, which will help me aim better."

The most important information Jackson has learned in his many years of turkey hunting is that choosing a place to take a stand for turkeys is one of the most critical keys for success.

"Every time I walk through the woods, whether I'm deer hunting or turkey hunting, I'm trying to see where the best spot will be to take a stand if I hear a turkey gobble," Jackson explains. "One of the worst things that can happen to a turkey hunter is to be caught in a particular area of the woods and have to set up because the turkey is too close or coming too fast for him to have time to set up a stand.

"Knowing how to pick the best spot from which to call a turkey is the most important aspect of being successful in turkey hunting. When I'm searching for a site to set up, I look behind myself. Then I can know what the turkey sees when he's coming to me. Many younger hunters look for a spot in front of themselves or on either side of themselves and don't see what the turkey will when he comes to them. They often choose a bad place from which to call. I make sure I have somewhere to hide so the turkey never will see me as he approaches."

Jackson believes the longer he hunts turkeys, the better he's able to hunt turkeys.

"I still can outwalk most 40-year-old turkey hunters, especially those with the big bellies," Jackson mentions as he chuckles. "I'll

*Patient, relaxed hunters become much better turkey hunters with each season.*

stay with a turkey much longer now and have more fun hunting him than I once did. If I have to spend a week on one turkey to be able to take him, then I don't mind investing that week in hunting that bird. But a younger hunter may leave that contrary turkey after one or two days of hunting him and go looking for a gobbler that's more aggressive that will come in easier."

By being more patient, more relaxed and having more knowledge, Jackson has become a much better turkey hunter than he ever has been at any other time of his life.

Many lessons can be learned from the master woodsmen who have spent decades hunting wily gobblers. I believe the greatest lesson we've all learned from these three masters of the sport is that the Good Lord in His infinite wisdom has saved the best turkey hunting for a time when we'll be old enough to appreciate it.

# INDEX

# FISHING & HUNTING
# RESOURCE DIRECTORY

# If you are interested in more productive fishing and hunting trips, then this info is for you!

Larsen's Outdoor Publishing is the publisher of several quality Outdoor Libraries - all informational-type books that focus on how and where to catch America's most popular sport fish, hunt America's most popular big game or travel to productive or exciting destinations.

The perfect-bound, soft-cover books include numerous illustrative

graphics, line drawings, maps and photographs. The BASS SERIES LIBRARY and the two HUNTING LIBRARIES are nationwide in scope. The INSHORE SERIES covers coastal areas from Texas to Maryland and foreign waters. The OUTDOOR TRAVEL SERIES covers the most popular fishing and diving destinations in the world. The BASS WATERS SERIES focuses on the top lakes and rivers in the nation's most visited largemouth bass fishing state.

All series appeal to outdoorsmen/readers of all skill levels. The unique four-color cover design, interior layout, quality, information content and economical price makes these books hot sellers in the marketplace. Best of all, you can learn to be more successful in your outdoor endeavors!!

# THE BASS SERIES LIBRARY
### by Larry Larsen

1. **FOLLOW THE FORAGE FOR BETTER BASS ANGLING VOL. 1 BASS/PREY RELATIONSHIP**

   Learn how to determine the dominant forage in a body of water, and you will consistently catch more and larger bass. Whether you fish artificial lures or live bait, your bass stringer will benefit!

2. **FOLLOW THE FORAGE FOR BETTER BASS ANGLING VOL. 2 TECHNIQUES**

   Learn why one lure or bait is more successful than others and how to use each lure under varying conditions. You will also learn highly productive patterns that will catch bass under most circumstances!

3. **BASS PRO STRATEGIES**

   Professional fishermen know how changes in pH, water temperature, color and fluctuations affect bass fishing, and they know how to adapt to weather and topographical variations. Learn from their experience. Your productivity will improve after spending a few hours with this compilation of tactics!

4. **BASS LURES - TRICKS & TECHNIQUES**

   When bass become accustomed to the same artificials and presentations seen over and over again, they become harder to catch. Learn how to rig or modify your lures and develop specific presentation and retrieve methods to spark or renew the interest of largemouth!

5. **SHALLOW WATER BASS**

   Bass spend 90% of their time in the shallows, and you spend the majority of the time fishing for them in waters less than 15 feet deep. Learn specific productive tactics that you can apply to fishing in marshes, estuaries, reservoirs, lakes, creeks and small ponds. You'll likely triple your results!

# THE BASS SERIES LIBRARY
## by Larry Larsen

### 6. BASS FISHING FACTS

Learn why and how bass behave during pre- and post-spawn, how they utilize their senses and how they respond to their environment, and you'll increase your bass angling success! This angler's guide to the lifestyles and behavior of the black bass is a reference source never before compiled. It examines how bass utilize their senses to feed. By applying this knowledge, your productivity will increase for largemouth as well as Redeye, Suwannee, Spotted and other bass species.

### 7. TROPHY BASS

If you're more interested in wrestling with one or two monster largemouth than with a "panfull" of yearlings, then learn what techniques and habitats will improve your chances. This book takes a look at geographical areas and waters that offer better opportunities to catch giant bass, as well as proven methods and tactics for both man made and natural waters. The "how to" information was gleaned from professional guides and other experienced trophy bass hunters.

### 8. ANGLER'S GUIDE TO BASS PATTERNS

Catch bass every time out by learning how to develop a productive pattern quickly and effectively. Learn the most effective combination of lures, methods and places. Understanding bass movement and activity and the most appropriate and effective techniques to employ will add many pounds of enjoyment to the sport of bass fishing.

### 9. BASS GUIDE TIPS

Learn the most productive methods of top bass fishing guides in the country and secret techniques known only in a certain region or state that may work in your waters. Special features include shiners, sunfish kites & flies; flippin, pitchin' & dead stickin' rattlin; skippin' & jerk baits; moving, deep, hot & cold waters; fronts, high winds & rain. New approaches for bass angling success!

# INSHORE SERIES
## by Frank Sargeant

**IL1. THE SNOOK BOOK**
"Must" reading for anyone who loves the pursuit of this unique sub-tropic species. Every aspect of how you can find and catch big snook is covered, in all seasons and all waters where snook are found.

**IL2. THE REDFISH BOOK**
Packed with expertise from the nation's leading redfish anglers and guides, this book covers every aspect of finding and fooling giant reds. You'll learn secret techniques revealed for the first time.

**IL3. THE TARPON BOOK**
Find and catch the wily "silver king" along the Gulf Coast, north through the mid-Atlantic, and south along Central and South American coastlines. Numerous experts share their most productive techniques.

**IL4. THE TROUT BOOK - *COMING SOON!***
You'll learn the best seasons, techniques and lures in this comprehensive book.

# OUTDOOR TRAVEL SERIES
## by Timothy O'Keefe and Larry Larsen

A candid guide with inside information on the best charters, time of the year, and other vital recommendations that can make your next fishing and/or diving trip much more enjoyable.

**OT1. FISH & DIVE THE CARIBBEAN - Volume 1**
Northern Caribbean, including Cozumel, Caymans Bahamas, Virgin Islands and other popular destinations.

**OT2. FISH & DIVE THE CARIBBEAN - Volume 2 - *COMING SOON!*** Southern Caribbean, including Guadeloupe, Bonaire, Costa Rica, Venezuela and other destinations.

# DEER HUNTING LIBRARY

### by John E. Phillips

**DH1. MASTERS' SECRETS OF DEER HUNTING**
Increase your deer hunting success significantly by learning from the masters of the sport. New information on tactics and strategies for bagging deer is included in this book, the most comprehensive of its kind.

**DH2. THE SCIENCE OF DEER HUNTING -** *COMING SOON!*

# TURKEY HUNTING LIBRARY

### by John E. Phillips

**TH1. MASTERS' SECRETS OF TURKEY HUNTING**
Masters of the sport have solved some of the most difficult problems you will encounter while hunting wily longbeards with bows, blackpowder guns and shotguns. Learn 10 deadly sins of turkey hunting and what to do if you commit them.

**TH2. OUTSMART TOUGH TURKEYS -** *COMING SOON!*

# BASS WATERS SERIES

### by Larry Larsen

Take the guessing game out of your next bass fishing trip. The most productive bass waters in each region of the state are described in this multi-volume series, including boat ramp information, seasonal tactics, water characteristics and much more. Popular and overlooked lakes, rivers, streams, ponds, canals, marshes and estuaries are clearly detailed with numerous maps and drawings.

**BW1. GUIDE TO NORTH FLORIDA BASS WATERS**
From Orange Lake north and west.

**BW2. GUIDE TO CENTRAL FLORIDA BASS WATERS**
From Tampa/Orlando to Palatka.

**BW3. GUIDE TO SOUTH FLORIDA BASS WATERS**
*COMING SOON!* - from I-4 to the Everglades.

# WRITE US!

By the way, if our books have helped you be more productive in your outdoor endeavors, we'd like to hear from you. Let us know which book or series has strongly benefited you and how it has aided your success or enjoyment.

We might be able to use the information in a future book. Such information is also valuable to our planning future titles and expanding on those already available.

Simply write to: Larry Larsen, Publisher, Larsen's Outdoor Publishing, 2640 Elizabeth Place, Lakeland, FL 33813.

We appreciate your comments!

*Larry Larsen*

## Save Money on Your Next Outdoor Book!

Because you've purchased a Larsen's Outdoor Publishing Book, you can be placed on our growing list of preferred customers.

● You can receive special discounts on our wide selection of Bass Fishing, Saltwater Fishing, Hunting, Outdoor Travel and other economically-priced books written by our expert authors.

### PLUS...

● Receive Substantial Discounts for Multiple Book Purchases! And...advance notices on upcoming books!

Send in your name TODAY to be added to our mailing list

___ Yes, put my name on your mailing list to receive:

1. Advance notice on **upcoming outdoor books.**
2. Special **discount offers.**

Name_____

Address_____

City/State/Zip_____

**Send to: Larsen's Outdoor Publishing, Special Offers, 2640 Elizabeth Place, Lakeland, FL 33813**

# LARSEN'S OUTDOOR PUBLISHING
## CONVENIENT ORDER FORM
### (All Prices Include Postage & Handling)

**BASS SERIES LIBRARY** - only $11.95 each or $79.95 for autographed set.

_____ 1.  Better Bass Angling - Vol. 1- Bass/Prey Interaction
_____ 2.  Better Bass Angling - Vol. 2 - Techniques
_____ 3.  Bass Pro Strategies
_____ 4.  Bass Lures - Tricks & Techniques
_____ 5.  Shallow Water Bass
_____ 6.  Bass Fishing Facts
_____ 7.  Trophy Bass
_____ 8.  Angler's Guide to Bass Patterns
_____ 9.  Bass Guide Tips

> **BIG SAVINGS!**
> Order 1 book, discount 5%
> 2 -3 books, discount 10%.
> 4 or more books discount 20%.

**INSHORE SERIES** - only $11.95 each

_____ IL1.  The Snook Book
_____ IL2.  The Redfish Book
_____ IL3.  The Tarpon Book

**DEER HUNTING SERIES** - only $11.95 each

_____ DH1.  Masters' Secrets of Deer Hunting

**TURKEY HUNTING SERIES** - only $11.95 each

_____ TH1.  Masters' Secrets of Turkey Hunting

**OUTDOOR TRAVEL SERIES** - only $13.95 each

_____ OT1.  Fish & Dive the Caribbean Vol 1 - Northern Caribbean

**BASS WATERS SERIES** - only $14.95 each

_____ BW1.  Guide To North Florida Bass Waters
_____ BW2.  Guide To Central Florida Bass Waters


NAME _____

ADDRESS _____

CITY_____STATE_____ZIP_____

No. of books ordered _____ x $_____ each =    _____
No. of books ordered _____ x $_____ each =    _____
                      Discount          =    _____

TOTAL ENCLOSED (Check or Money Order)    $_____

### Copy this page and mail to:
### Larsen's Outdoor Publishing, Dept. RD91
### 2640 Elizabeth Place, Lakeland, FL 33813

*Image Size 15" X 23"*  ## TREETOP GOBBLER

### ABOUT THE ARTIST

At age 25, Eddie LeRoy of Eufaula, Alabama, is considered one of the most talented and potentially great wildlife artists in the country. He has won the Alabama Wildlife Federation's 1989-90 Art Competition, the 1990-91 Florida Wild Turkey Stamp Competition and placed in the top nine in the National Wild Turkey Federation Competition. LeRoy was chosen by Waterfowl U.S.A. to be the 1990-91 sponsored Print Artist of the Year. LeRoy is also an ardent angler and proficient hunter.

LeRoy's original paintings and prints steadily have grown in value each year - a wise investment for the outdoor sportsman. His work has appeared in "Deer and Deer Hunting," "Hunter's World," "Buckmasters," "Alabama Conservation," "Alabama Wildlife," "Turkey Call," "B.A.S.S. Masters" and "Southern Outdoors" magazines and Aqua-Field Publications.

Printed on acid-free paper, the cost is $45 per print, plus $5 for shipping and handling for a total of $50.

**Send check or money order to:**
**Night Hawk Publications**
**P.O. Drawer 375, Fairfield, AL 35064**
**We accept Master Card or Visa**
**Call Toll Free 1-800-627-HAWK (4295)**
**Please allow four weeks for delivery**